T0358708

On Marx

KEY CRITICAL THINKERS IN EDUCATION

Series Editors:

Michael A. Peters
University of Illinois at Urbana-Champaign, USA

Tina (A. C.) Besley
California State University, San Bernardino, USA

Scope:

This series is an edition dedicated to the revival of the critical approaches of key thinkers whose thought has strongly influenced and shaped educational theory: Rousseau, Marx, Gramsci, Dewey, Marcuse, Rogers, Freire, Derrida, Foucault, Said and Butler. In this first edition the series includes eleven monographs in total, each approximately sixty pages long with three chapters, a brief introduction, a bibliographical essay, a glossary and series of study questions. The aim is designed to provide cheap and accessible texts for students that give clear accounts of these thinkers and their significance for educational theory. The monographs are written by a group of internationally renown scholars whose own work embodies the critical ethos.

On Marx:
An Introduction to the Revolutionary Intellect of Karl Marx

Paula Allman
Nottingham, UK

SENSE PUBLISHERS
ROTTERDAM / TAIPEI

ISBN 978-90-8790-192-9 (paperback)
ISBN 978-90-8790-193-6 (hardback)

Published by: Sense Publishers,
P.O. Box 21858, 3001 AW Rotterdam, The Netherlands

http://www.sensepublishers.com

Printed on acid-free paper

To Tippity, P.K. & Tabitha
(for their unrelenting love and support as well as their equally unrelenting pestering)

TABLE OF CONTENTS

SERIES FOREWORD

It is entirely fitting that Paula Allman's book *On Marx: An Introduction to the Revolutionary Intellect of Karl Marx* should be the first in our new series Key Critical Thinkers in Education. Who better could grace the opening of the series and who else has better claim to the mantle of 'key critical thinker'. Marx has to be reinvented and reread for each new generation. As Foucault suggests, Marx like Freud and Nietzsche is 'a figure of discursivity' meaning that Marx's work founded a discursive tradition that is both rich and complex and is to be measured by the number of novel interpretations and and readings it generates. By this measure there is no doubt that Marx's approach from radical political economy to capital and capitalism has as much relevance today as it had when Marx was writing in the mid-nineteenth century even if the basis of industrial capitalism has begun to shift and we now hear talk of the 'knowledge economy'. His critical orientation is significant in that every major thinker interested in political economy or social and cultural history must either adopt a sympathetic framework or differentiate themselves against Marx.

We can think of nobody better than Paula Allman to author the first in our series. Paula Allman has been actively involved in critical education for many years. Paula has written extensively on Freire and Gramsci, and she has contributed a number of books to the critical tradition including *Revolutionary Social Transformation: Democratic Hopes, Political Possibilities and Critical Education* (1999) and *Critical Education Against Global Capital: Karl Marx and Revolutionary Critical Education* (2001). Her approach to Marx in this critical text is to focus on capital/capitalism, consciousness, and education—three topics that comprise the main body of the book, which together with a bibliographical essay defines the concept behind the series.

As the general editors, we decided to develop a series on Key Critical Thinkers in Education for a number of reasons. First, we wanted to develop this series as a counterpoint to an emerging form of research in the field of education that acquiesces in the face of power and growing inequalities. This is a form of research that underlies prevalent notions of science in the U.S. and U.K.—generally it tries hard to emulate the hard sciences choosing as its model third-generation cognitive or brain science or medical science where answers are sought 'internally' and individually rather than culturally, historically or socially, and policies and programs are designed as 'interventions'. Such science is oriented to longitudinal studies, evidence-based, experimental or double-blind, and best-practice. It is based on the out-dated assumptions that science progresses gradually through the accumulation of 'data' or information and mostly it is funded by government agencies, which means it takes a reactive form, sticking to the evaluation of existing programs or policies. It is as though the historical and social studies of science initiated by Thomas Kuhn in 1962 with the launch of *The Structure of Scientific Revolutions* has meant nothing. Against this State-funded revival of the worst sort of crude positivism that now motivates the university in its search of research dollars, we sought to remind the next generation of students in education that there have been critical thinkers in the field of education and their thought is still relevant.

Second, we want to signal that the critical tradition counts amongst its members many different thinkers that have come to us from a range of disciplines: political economy, politics, philosophy, counseling, sociology, history, and literature. The first eleven books in the series serve to elucidate the thought of Rousseau, Marx, Gramsci, Dewey, Freire, Rogers, Marcuse, Foucault, Derrida, Said and Butler.

Third, we decided to develop a series that provided short introductions to these key critical thinkers through an easy-to-read format that whetted the appetite and also made available a bibliographical essay for additional reading and study. Each chapter, restricted in size and scope, highlights important terms in the text that are incorporated in a glossary, and ends with a set of questions. The aim then is to be student-friendly in providing accessible but brief and authoritative introductions that can be read at one sitting.

We wish to congratulate Paula Allman on her excellent introduction to Marx and to invite you to settle back with this text for a few hours of stimulating commentary, scholarship and analysis.

Michael A Peters & Tina (A.C.) Besley
San Bernardino, California
May, 2007

ACKNOWLEDGEMENTS

There are never sufficient words to express gratitude to the family and friends who are my constant support. For the sake of brevity on this occasion, I trust that a sincerely heart-felt thank-you will do. There are, however, some of these people who deserve to be specifically acknowledged for their contributions to this book. I thank Glenn Rikowski and Gordon Alderink for reading and commenting on an early draft of Chapter 1; Rachel Gorman, Shahrzad Mojab and Deb Hill for their ongoing and valuable support for and contributions to my work as well as their contributions to critical education theory, research and practice and Jill Vincent, who always goes above and beyond what even the dearest friends should do, for proof-reading and commenting on the entire book. The support and help of all of these friends has been invaluable. I also owe a special debt of gratitude to Peter Mayo who put the series Editors in touch with me. Peter, another close friend and formidable Freirean/Gramscian scholar, is the person initially responsible for the publication of my three books; and I am deeply indebted to him.

I also thank the series editors, Michael Peters and Tina Besley for inviting me to contribute *On Marx* to their series and also for their foresight in recognising the need for an introductory series of this nature. In addition, I want to acknowledge and thank Peter de Liefde, of Sense Publications, for his valuable assistance throughout this project.

Last and far from least, I am extremely indebted to Karl Marx who has consistently stimulated my thinking for the past quarter of a century, and who enabled me to understand why so many of our brothers and sisters across the globe suffer, why there is no need for the continuation of this suffering and what must be done to bring their suffering to an end. The quality of our lives and our own humanity is co-dependent on the quality of theirs; to paraphrase both Marx and Paolo Freire, we can not be fully human unless and until they are.

INTRODUCTION

In 1999, on the eve of the new millennium, participants in a BBC poll voted Karl Marx the "greatest thinker" of the second millennium. It was neither the first nor the last accolade to this prodigious thinker. Humanity was always Marx's primary concern. In this apologetically brief introduction to Marx's thought, two of his greatest contributions to our understanding of the human condition are explored along with the implications of his thought for education. Ironically and regrettably, far too much of Marx's celebrity derives from myths, erroneous attributions, misunderstandings and misinterpretations, and far too little relates to his real genius. This book attempts to deal with that real genius, but first it is important to mention two of the most widespread errors of attribution. Many people assume that Marx was the founder of socialism/communism. Moreover, they assume that his ideas provided a theoretical blueprint for 20th Century, socialist/communist revolutions and societies. Socialism and communism pre-date Marx, and although he was critical of the various theories pertaining to these forms of socio-economic organisation, he, in fact, wrote very little about how socialism/communism would actually work. One can glean a vision from his writings but one that is based on ideals or goals for humanity's progressive development not one that specifies particulars. To do so would have been contradictory for Marx because he believed those struggling to create these societies would democratically establish the particulars. As a consequence, due to their undemocratic character, most 20th Century forms of socialism/communism would have been an anathema to him. The majority of Marx's writing involves a critique of capitalism, bourgeois society and liberal democracy—the political form of governance most conducive to the growth and maintenance of capitalism. The point, here, is that in undertaking this exploration of Marx's critical thought, it is important to suspend, for the duration, any previously held assumptions and to critically assess what he actually thought. To get inside critical thinkers' ideas, it helps to consider the factors that may have influenced and motivated them. I begin, therefore, with a succinct description of the social/historical context within which Marx's thinking developed and came to maturity.

Marx was born on May 5, 1818 in Trier, an ancient town located in the Rhineland region of Germany. Although he was born into an orthodox Jewish family, his early influences were of French origin, viz., French rationalist philosophy, romanticism, the French Enlightenment and Revolution. France, under Napoleon, had occupied Trier from 1803-1818, and Marx's father had been so taken by French liberal ideas that he abandoned his Judaism. The French influence came not only from Marx's father; between 1820 and 1830, the entire Rhineland was inundated with both liberal and socialist ideas, many of which originated in France. Moreover, Ludwig von Westphalen, a Saint-Simonian socialist, was the young Marx's mentor (and also his future father-in-law). He was considerably more radical than the other adults in Marx's life, and it was probably through the writings of Saint-Simon that Marx first became aware of the oppression of the proletariat. Although Marx, himself, never became a Saint-Simonian and remained critical of all the new socialist/communist thinking, he nevertheless was sympathetic with their sentiments, especially their humanism. At University, in Berlin, it was his concern for the proletariat, the poorest and most numerous group in capitalist societies, that prompted his critique of Hegel's philosophy and that also eventually led Marx to join and give a new direction to the socialist movement.

Until the early 1840's, Marx's critiques were of a philosophical nature. He found fault with any philosopher or political figure that failed to grasp the relationship between the ideals being espoused and the real world. Marx developed his own distinctive social theory through a process that often involved first embracing and then critically engaging with the thinking of others, in particular Hegel and Feuerbach. In each case, he retained the aspects he deemed valid, for example, Hegel's dialectical conceptualisation, while moving beyond it in the pursuit of truth and a politics that could lead to human emancipation.

Marx fell in love with and married Jenny von Westphalen, the daughter of his early mentor. This union provided him with a lifelong loving companion, but also, and especially as their family grew, with the unrelenting necessity of making a living. His radical ideas prevented him from working as either a university academic or a lawyer—the professions for which he was qualified. The remaining alternative was journalism, but here too there were problems. His radical ideas often increased circulation, but without fail this would, in turn, gain the attention of the government censors. Repeatedly, Marx would find himself unemployed and soon after exiled first from Germany, and subsequently from both Paris and Brussels.

Although Marx first met Frederick Engels, his lifelong friend, collaborator and frequent financial supporter, in Cologne in 1842, it was their journalistic endeavours in Paris in 1843-44 that brought the two together and that afforded Marx the benefit of a colleague who shared his thinking and his aspirations for humanity. Engels brought to the relationship not just loyalty and an appreciation of Marx's intellect (Wheen, 2000) but also an in-depth practical knowledge of capitalist industry and the actual conditions of the industrial working class.

Europe was in turmoil during the 1840's, and so too was Marx's life. The decade was marked by increasing radicalism and attempted revolutions that invariably led to counter-revolutions and suppression by conservative forces. Exile propelled the Marx family first to Paris, then Brussels, as mentioned before, and eventually, after brief returns to both Germany and Paris, the Marx family came to London in 1849, where, at last, they found a permanent home. In each of these locations, Marx read and wrote voraciously, and, with equal enthusiasm, he also engaged in endless political discussions, meetings and activities. It was in Paris, in the early 1840's, that he first began his study of political economy. At this time, the theories of various bourgeois economists such as James Mill, David Ricardo and Adam Smith were the focus of his critical scrutiny. This study, enriched by Engel's account of the real world of industrial capitalism, culminated in the *Economic and Philosophical Manuscripts* of 1843-44, the work that marks Marx's transition from philosophical criticism to critical socio-economic theorist (Bottomore, 1988). By 1848, when he and Engels published the first edition of the *Communist Manifesto*, Marx had committed himself to the proletariat, the class that he believed would bring about the full emancipation of humanity, and equally, he had committed himself to developing a comprehensive and critical understanding of capitalism. He knew that this understanding would be an essential theoretical weapon for the working class in their struggle to abolish capitalism.

Marx's proximity to the British Museum, throughout the 1850's, was to prove invaluable. By law, every book, journal, pamphlet, report and magazine published in Britain had to be deposited in the Museum (now the British Library); therefore, Marx was able to access unrivalled resources on his topic of interest, capitalism. These resources also included a new type of source, viz., the statistical data reported by the newly appointed official commissions of inquiry that had been set up to investigate the adverse effects of capitalism on working class lives. It must be remembered that capitalism was a relatively new phenomenon that developed and first reached maturity in England. By the end of his life, Marx probably knew more about the history of British political economy than professors of the subject (Briggs, 1982). Until the last few years of the decade, Marx's studies were frequently interrupted by the necessity of earning a living. As always, his main source of income, besides the financial support he received from Engels, came from journalism—at this time, mainly from the articles he regularly contributed to the *New York Daily Tribune*. Despite the interruptions and the frustration that accompanied them, by the end of the 1850's, Marx had achieved his goal. In today's vernacular, he had "outed" capitalism and had already begun to share his findings with the world. Between 1857 and 1867, he penned the various volumes of his critical political economy—volumes that explain capital and capitalism with a precision and depth of analysis and insight that have never since been equalled. It is important to emphasise that no matter how engrossed Marx became with his study and writing, he always remained in touch with both political and economic developments in the real world of capitalism. Karl Marx died in London in 1883, just fifteen months after the death of his beloved Jenny. They were survived by only two of their six children. Incessant poverty had taken its toll on the Marx family.

In the remaining pages of this introduction, Marx's unique paradigm of critical thinking, his dialectical conceptualisation, is explained. It is this form of conceptualising that gives Marx's analytical critique unparalleled sagacity and strength. Armed with at least an initial understanding of dialectical conceptualisation, readers will be able to more easily and accurately comprehend Marx's explanations. I also briefly discuss some of the concepts that are frequently involved in misinterpretations of Marx's writings. In Chapter 1, I offer a comprehensive summary of Marx's analytical critique of capital and capitalism. I explain his theory of consciousness in Chapter 2, and in Chapter 3, I consider the impact of Marxist theory on education and the educational implications that can be drawn from Marx's thought. Each chapter contains a brief summary and a few questions for further study or reflection. At the end of the book, readers will find, in addition to the indexed references, a bibliographical essay and a glossary/index. Despite his best efforts, many of Marx's most important writings were not published until after his death and in some cases long after his death. Since this can lead to confusion, references to Marx's writings in this text follow a convention adopted from Derek Sayer (Sayer, 1987). The first date in these references pertains to the date when Marx last worked on a text prior to its first publication, and the second date is the date of the published source that I have consulted. In addition, whenever it is important for readers to know the exact place in a source from which a particular point comes, I cite the page number even when I have not directly quoted the source.

Readers may wonder why Marx is relevant to educators. If you agree that teaching and education must be about much more than the transfer of knowledge from teachers to students, that it involves enabling learners to develop the ability to think critically and the ability to understand the world well enough that they can begin to shape their own destinies and with others the progressive development of humanity, then Marx is for you. I envy those of you who are just beginning your educational vocation. It was comparatively late in my career when I first came to Marx; whereas your journey into understanding Marx and our world can begin right here. My aim is to ease the preliminary stages of that journey as much as possible. Marx is not easy, but I trust you will find that he is worth every ounce of sincere and serious effort on both your part and mine.

MARX'S DIALECTICAL CONCEPTUALISATION

As mentioned previously, to discover and then expose the truth of capitalism, Marx employed a specific type of critical thinking—actually, a new paradigm of critical thought. Marx's dialectical conceptualisation is not a method, in the strict sense of that word. In other words, it is not an abstract, formal, step-by-step approach but rather a manner of intellectually grasping the truth, or the internal structure/essence, of any real phenomenon, which is not transparently obvious or observable. To explain this process, or what I have called Marx's dialectical conceptualisation, first the general or prevailing assumptions that constitute his critical orientation are considered and then the inter-related conceptual tools he employs are explained. Although I have created these two divisions and discuss the features of the critical orientation and the conceptual tools separately because language does not permit me to do otherwise, it is important to emphasise that the entire process of dialectical conceptualisation is inter-related, thus all components work together as an integrated paradigm of critical thinking. Furthermore, Marx's specific form of dialectical conceptualisation is a paradigm of thought that arises from a historically specific reality—a paradigm of thought, therefore, which is absolutely essential for grasping and fully comprehending the truth of that reality.

Marx's Critical Orientation

One of the most important assumptions, which Marx employs either explicitly or implicitly throughout his writings, is that the focus of his analysis pertains to **historically specific** phenomena. As a consequence, any truth discovered is also historically specific. This involves making a distinction between that which is transhistorical, or applicable to the entirety of human history, and that which arises in a particular form within a specific socio-economic formation, or organisation of society. Marx assumes that any truth treated as transhistorical should be viewed with suspicion. Often, when such truth is found, it is so general or lacking in substance that it is virtually useless for critical purposes. As a consequence, transhistorical truth is not a proper objective for intellectual inquiry into social and economic phenomena; it has no critical purchase on the reality it purports to depict, which can advance our critical understanding of that reality. Therefore, it is important to bear in mind that in all of Marx's writings his explanations and critical discussions, whether of scientific laws, the state, democracy or whatever, are historically specific to capitalism.

Throughout this book, I emphasise the dialectical nature of Marx's critical thought, but in no way is this intended to diminish the importance of its historical dimension. In fact, one of the key features of Marx's critical orientation, a feature that is a recurring theme, is the relation between **preconditions and results**. In his explanations of capital and capitalism, he repeatedly refers to the preconditions that lay the foundations for and that develop into specific results. Certain results, in turn, become the preconditions for more highly developed, more complex, results. Marx provides readers with a wealth of historical evidence that traces the movement from precondition to result. There is no predetermined, or teleological, end to this process. However, when Marx reveals the embryonic form of the result, one can understand how the subsequent unfolding of the precondition is both logical and historical. In other words, the sequence of development follows a logic that is internal to the phenomenon and which can only come to fruition through human agency within historical time.

In the three volumes of *Capital*, Marx explains how the **essence** of capital develops into **appearance**, i.e., our everyday, very real, experience of the concrete and complex reality of a fully developed capitalist socio-economic formation. In Volumes 1 and 2, Marx's critical analysis unveils the essence of capital as well as its historical development. He begins this explanation, in Volume 1, by depicting his dialectical conceptualisation of a commodity because this is the form, or result, through which all of us most frequently experience the relations of capitalism. Moreover, the development of the products of human labour into commodities is also an essential precondition for the advent of capitalism. This development and the development of the entire essence are discussed in Chapter 1 of this book. The overall objective of Volume 1 is to explain how the development of the commodity form results in establishing the historically specific social relations of capitalist production. In Volume 2, Marx completes his explication of capital's essence by analysing the human activities that take place in the circulation and exchange of commodities and by establishing the relation between these activities and the production relations of capitalism. Finally, in Volume 3, he explains how the essence operates, how it manifests in observable results, in the concrete, complex totality of capitalism where there are many capitalist firms in competition with one another. In other words, the movement or process Marx discovered in his analysis of capitalist reality is explained as movement from essence to appearance and within that historically specific process as movement from preconditions to results. To avoid confusion later, it is important to mention the fourth volume of *Capital*. During the same span of years that Marx wrote the 3 volumes of *Capital*, he also wrote a separate 3 volume text entitled *Theories of Surplus Value* in which he critically analyses the way in which both bourgeois and socialist political economists thought about and understood capital and capitalism. I include myself as one who considers these 3 volumes to be integrally related to the 3 volumes of *Capital* and therefore its fourth volume. Why this is the case, will become clear in Chapter 2 of this text when Marx's theory of consciousness is discussed.

The final feature of Marx's critical orientation involves his understanding of the meaning and purpose of **science**. Even though there are aspects of Marx's science that are unique, there are other aspects that are shared by anyone engaged in scientific endeavours. However, Marx's concept of science, like that of most other scientists, differs fundamentally from the concept of science normally prevalent in common sense. This is particularly the case when a statement is designated as a scientific law. In common sense, or lay thinking, these laws are often thought to be immutable truths. To counter this notion, it is instructive to consider the general features of any scientific approach to understanding, including Marx's.

During the initial stage of scientific inquiry, scientists formulate abstractions that they cull from observations of the phenomenon/a under investigation and from thinking about these observations. After further thinking and observation, some of these abstractions are specified in the form of hypotheses and/or null hypotheses. These are predictions that often refer to unobservable phenomenon/a, which scientists suspect may be the cause, or essence, of the phenomenon/a they have been observing. Next, experiments are conducted or further evidence is collected so that the predictions/hypotheses can either be accepted or rejected. Sometimes these endeavours result in the discovery of a scientific fact or, more momentously, a scientific law. When the latter type of finding is formalised in writing, the statement specifies how some phenomenon/a works or how it came into existence under defined conditions, which include the absence of certain extraneous variables. This is the same scientific process to which Marx adhered. He tested the abstractions he had formulated from observation and thought against the economic data and theory he collected during his long hours of study at the British Museum. Moreover, whenever he states an economic law of capitalism, he also identifies the counteracting influences, or the factors that can impede the systematic operation of the law—often not just thwarting but also even reversing its regular operation.

However, Marx's science does differ from other scientific practice in one very fundamental way, which is directly connected to his assumption of historical specificity. When facts or even laws are discovered in other areas of science, they are considered to be transhistorical. In other words, they were true before they were discovered and always will be true. Marx's discoveries pertain exclusively to the 'hidden essence' of capital and capitalism and the way in which this essence appears and is experienced in the concrete reality of capitalism. The laws that Marx explicates identify the factors, which govern the movement and development of capital. Therefore, Marx's science is historically specific to capitalism and will be of only historical interest once capitalism is abolished. Marx needed his dialectical science, based on dialectical conceptualisation, because capitalism's conditions of possibility are far from obvious or transparent. As part of his dialectical conceptualisation, Marx employed certain conceptual tools that enabled his intellect to penetrate the appearance, the surface reality of capitalism, in order to discover and lay bare the essence of capital.

Marx's Conceptual Tools

To reiterate, although each concept is discussed in sequence, they, together with the features of Marx's critical orientation, should be understood as an inter-related totality. Together they constitute Marx's dialectical conceptualisation—his unique paradigm of critical thought. The first concept, **internal relations**, is so crucial to Marx's thought that his entire system of thinking has been referred to as 'a philosophy of internal relations' (Ollman, 1976). Although this concept is central to Marx's thinking, I contend that his dialectical conceptualisation also involves the other dimensions discussed here. Generally speaking, the ability to conceptualise, or to form concepts, is a necessary element of human thinking because concepts enable us to organise and make sense of the plethora of evidence we encounter each day. Conceptualising, or thinking, in terms of internal relations is a particular form of relational as opposed to categorical thinking. Categorical thinking is the simplest, and on occasion a sufficient, form of conceptualisation, and a great deal of scientific practice uses or has developed from the use of categorisation. Intellectually organising the natural world into plants and animals or the physical world into solids, liquids and gases enhances our understanding and aids the scientific investigation of these phenomena. Categorisation involves discovering the attributes that distinguish one category from another. Sometimes, however, there is a need to develop more complex understandings, e.g., conceptualising phenomena in their relations with other phenomena. For this level of understanding we need relational conceptualisation.

There are two types of relational thinking. Conceptualising phenomena in their external relations is the most common, least complex, but sometimes sufficient, type of relational thought. It involves focussing on the result that occurs when two or more phenomena interact with one another. With this type of relational thought, the only perceived change is the result of the interaction. The pre-existing attributes of the interacting phenomena are not perceived as changing. Moreover, the result is a new phenomenon with no necessary or essential connection for its survival to the phenomena from which it emerged.

Conceptualising categorically or in terms of external relations is not sufficient, however, when it comes to developing an accurate understanding of certain complex phenomena. For these, it is necessary to conceptualise phenomenon/a as internally related to other phenomenon/a or as, themselves, the result of an internal relation. In this case, the result is necessarily and essentially related to the internally related phenomena from which it has emerged. In other words, its existence depends upon the ongoing existence of the original internal relation. Conceptualising in terms of internal relations involves focussing on the relation and how the attributes of the phenomena that are internally related are continually shaped and determined within the relation. Therefore, this is a very historical or developmental manner of conceptualising. Marx's analysis of capital's essence focuses on the internal relation between labour and capital, which is called the production relation, as well as the internal relation between the production relation and circulation/exchange.

There are many phenomena that can be conceptualised as internally related; however, Marx's critical analysis usually is directed at a particular type of internal relation, which he refers to as either a **dialectical contradiction** or a **unity of opposites**. He uses these terms synonymously sometimes also referring to dialectical contradictions as real contradictions in order to emphasise that they exist in the real world rather than erroneous thinking or irrational behaviour. It is important to consider the precise nature of a dialectical contradiction. As intimated above, a dialectical contradiction is an internally related unity of opposites, e.g., labour and capital, in which one of the opposites is called the positive in that its role is to preserve the relation; while the other opposite is the negative because its role eventually is to abolish the relation. This abolition is called the negation of the negation. Crucially, abolition involves the relation, and when the opposites are composed of human beings, it does not mean that they are abolished; however, the opposites, as opposites, will no longer exist. In the example of labour and capital, the negation of the negation means that labour will cease existing as a separate and oppressed class, bringing about the elimination of class divisions and the possibility of authentic human emancipation.

As mentioned previously, an internally related unity of opposites/dialectical contradiction may also produce a result. Marx calls this result a **form**. It was also mentioned before that unlike the result of an external relation, which once constituted has a separate existence from the phenomena that produced it, the form remains vitally connected to its source. Sometimes the form moves between the opposites effectively cementing the relation, or binding the opposites, and at other times, the form moves between the original internal relation and other relations, both internal and external. When Marx wants to signal that he is analysing the movement of a form, he calls the form a **mediation**. The value-form, which is discussed in detail in Chapter 1, arises from the labour-capital relation, binding labour and capital together in their inner-action with one another. It also moves between, and thus mediates, all the social relations and habituated practices of capitalism. In so doing the value-form binds all of these into the vast human network that is often referred to as the social structure of capitalism—a very human structure of social relations and practices in which people engage in order to produce their material existence. Of course laws, governments, institutions, etc. are created to give permanence to this structure of human relations, but it is important to remember that the substance of the structure is the sensuous activity of human beings. Obviously, people enter into all manner of social relations. However, Marx's focus was always the internally related social relations that underpin and constitute capitalism as a distinctive type of socio-economic organisation, i.e., social formation. It was these internal relations that made his dialectical conceptualisation necessary and which also figure centrally in his scientific explanation of capital and capitalism.

MAJOR MISINTERPRETATIONS OF MARX'S THOUGHT

Marx's unique paradigm of critical thinking, his dialectical conceptualisation, often has been ignored, and this has resulted in the past and continues unabated to result in misinterpretations of his concepts. In this final section, I offer a very cursory discussion of five concepts, which are often interpreted in a manner that is totally at odds with Marx's actual meaning. The meaning Marx attributes to these concepts is more fully explained in subsequent chapters.

Marx is all too frequently berated for failing to offer a clear concept of class. Not only is this accusation preposterous, the tendency to buy into it has lead many self-proclaimed Marxists to the erroneous assumption that the working class, the class dialectically opposed to capital, is comprised of only those people who engage in physical, or industrial/manual labour. Marx used various concepts to refer to the working class, or proletariat, the most important of which is productive labour. It is this term that he uses when referring to the unity of opposites that constitutes the labour-capital relation. Marx is very clear that productive does not refer to the production of a particular commodity or type of commodity but to the production of surplus-value, which is the source of capitalist profit. For Marx, class is not a thing, or socio-economic category; class is a relation, viz., the internal relation between labour and capital. Once this is understood, it is easy to see why Marx predicted the persistent growth, not the demise, of the working class. As capitalism grows into an increasingly global system, more and more workers in services and even the professions are drawn into the labour-capital relation thus becoming productive labour. For a very clear example wherein he actually refers to teachers, see (Marx, 1867:1976, p. 644).

When it comes to the concept of ideology, far too many Marxist and non-Marxist scholars take their lead from Lenin rather than Marx. According to Lenin, ideology is a system of beliefs that serves the interest of a particular class; therefore, besides, and opposed to, bourgeois ideology, there is working class, or proletarian, ideology. Ideology is discussed in depth in Chapter 2, but at this point, it is sufficient to state that for Marx, ideology is a negative concept, which refers to an uncritical, partial and fragmented mode of thinking that arises from human beings' sensuous activity within the social relations of capitalism (Larrain, 1983).

The social relations of capitalism is yet another frequently misconstrued concept. Numerous socialists and even some Marxists have thought and persist in thinking that Marx was speaking about property relations and thus the private ownership of property, especially the private ownership of the means of production. It has been mentioned previously in this Introduction that Marx's critical analysis focuses on the social relations that distinguish capitalism as a historically specific socio-economic formation, and these were the internal relations, which constitute the essence of capital and capitalism. According to Marx, private property and the unequal distribution of wealth result from capital's essence once capitalism is established. They also pre-date capitalism and served as preconditions for it coming into existence. Since they are not constitutive of capitalism, their abolition would not bring about the abolition of capitalism.

Far too many who claim to be adherents of Marx also incorrectly assume that the state, bourgeois state, and capitalist technology are neutral, and therefore they could be taken over by and used to the benefit of the working class. Once again, with an understanding of Marx's dialectical conceptualisation, and especially his concept of internal relations, it is clear that anything that has been created within the exploitative relations of capitalism, e.g., a state created to serve the interests of capital or machines designed to extract the maximum surplus labour from workers can hardly be neutral. If and when people abolish the social relations of capitalism and begin the process of creating a socially and economically just social formation, they will have to critically scrutinise almost everything developed within capitalist relations (e.g., Marx, 1872:1977). If found wanting, these elements would need to be transformed in accord with the new social relations, and this would pertain to much more than the state and technology, e.g., bourgeois forms of education, family and democracy.

Lastly, the idea that socialism/communism will inevitably develop out of capitalism, i.e., the historical inevitability of socialism/communism, is frequently attributed to Marx. It is true that some of Marx's speeches to working class audiences might have fostered this idea. After all, he was trying to rally and encourage the working class to engage in revolution. However, there is nothing in Marx's serious writing, e.g., his critical analysis of capitalism (all of which was written for a working class audience) that could be construed as corroborating this or any other type of teleological, deterministic notion. Moreover, there is a great deal of his writing that can be interpreted as a direct refutation of such thinking. Marx did think, however, that since socialism/communism would involve meeting the needs of all human beings, it would develop more quickly if established in capitalist societies that had served the historically progressive function of raising human productive abilities to an unprecedented degree. It was Rosa Luxembourg, the famous German revolutionary, who purportedly warned her comrades that capitalism was just as likely to develop into a sophisticated form of barbarism, as it was socialism/communism. Hopefully, the factors, which will be decisive in that outcome, will become clear in the chapters that follow.

MARX ON CAPITAL/CAPITALISM

To fully appreciate Marx's genius in revealing the 'hidden essence' of capital/capitalism as well as the way in which this essence develops into our contemporary experience of capitalism, one needs to follow his elucidation of the intricate unfolding of capital's internal relations and forms. I have offered a comprehensive synopsis of his full explanation elsewhere (Allman, 2001). In this text, space limitations preclude the inclusion of Marx's detailed historical and analytical proof of his assertions; instead I present only the bare essentials of the content presented in Volumes 1-3 of Marx's *Capital*. The essentials are then applied in a brief consideration of four of humanity's most ominous contemporary problems: credit and debt, globalisation, environmental destruction and poverty. This glimpse at the power of Marx's explanation to address some of our most important current concerns is meant to encourage readers to undertake their own study of Marx's writings. For those of you who are still wondering why educators need to understand Marx, let me elaborate on what I said previously. I have always contended, as reflected in this text, that educators, regardless of the subject/s they teach, need to understand the world in which they are preparing people to live and work. In the 21st Century, this world is the world of global capitalism, and Marx understood better than anyone else, to date, how this world works—how it moves and develops according to the inherent laws of capital.

Marx's exposition of his critical analysis of capital begins with an in-depth exploration of the commodity, or more precisely the commodity-form. This simple form is both the precondition for the advent of capitalism and the most pervasive result of fully developed capitalist societies. In pre-capitalist societies, commodity exchange only takes place on the periphery of society—in foreign or external trade. It is only with the full development of capitalism that commodity exchange becomes dominant and pervasive both within and between nations. Marx explains that every product of human labour is a use-value, i.e., it is useful in some way or another to the person who produces it and/or other people. The commodity, on the other hand, is an historically specific form of the product, a form with a dual nature. The commodity appears to be a unity of use-value and exchange-value. However, exchange-value is the form of appearance of value: therefore, the commodity is actually a unity of use-value and value, i.e., an internally related unity of opposites. Value and its objectified form, exchange-value, derive from the fact that the labour that produces a commodity also has a two-fold, or dual, nature. It is this dual nature, which allows for the exchange of commodities. A specific skill or technique of labour produces a specific use-value, but value and exchange-value can only exist on the basis of all commodities sharing something in common.

Clearly, the shared factor cannot be the concrete, or specific, labour that gives rise to their use-values. Marx demonstrates that the only possible shared factor is labour in general, or abstract labour, and also that this abstract, socially homogeneous labour is the substance of value. However, the only way to distinguish between the abstract labour in one as opposed to another commodity is by a quantitative measure of its duration, i.e., the magnitude of value contained in a commodity is determined by the labour-time expended in the production of this specific type of commodity. Of course, this cannot be the actual labour-time expended in the production of a particular commodity because that would mean that the least skilled and slowest worker would produce the most expensive, or most valuable, commodity of that type. According to Marx's Law of Value, "the magnitude of value", i.e., exchange-value, of any commodity is determined by the "labour-time socially necessary for its production." (Marx, 1867:1976, p. 129) By 'socially necessary labour-time', Marx means the time it takes to produce a particular type of commodity under the normal conditions that prevail at a particular time in a given society and to produce it with the average degree of skill and intensity prevalent in those normal conditions. To reiterate, the commodity's value underpins its exchange-value. The latter is the objectified form in which value appears when commodities are brought into relation with one another in exchange. Marx's Law of Value and his concept of socially necessary labour-time, which is a central component of this law, are extremely important, and although they are far from obvious in fully developed capitalist societies, they continuously shape and determine the way in which capitalist economies work.

As commodity trade develops, two very special commodities come into being. One of these commodities pre-dates capitalism but goes on to develop in very specific and sophisticated ways once capitalism is established. The other special commodity actually makes capitalism possible. The first is the money commodity, initially gold and silver. It is easy to think that the value of gold and silver emanates from their natural qualities and, consequently, to forget that both of these metals have to be extracted from the earth by human labour. Therefore, just like any other exchangeable product, i.e., commodity, the value of gold and/or silver is determined by the labour-time socially necessary for their production. The money commodity, or money-form of value, greatly facilitates and also accelerates trade. Instead of the value equivalency (exchange-value) of each commodity having to be established relative to the value of other commodities, the exchange-value of every commodity can be expressed relative to the value of the universal equivalent, money.

Labour-power is the second very special commodity, the commodity that actually makes capitalism possible (p. 270). Between the fifteenth and eighteenth centuries, the land from which the peasant population secured their subsistence was increasingly privatised. These people came to the point of having only one commodity, which they could sell in order to purchase the necessities of life. That commodity was their labour-power, the commodity that serves the same purpose for the vast majority of human beings in the 21st Century.

As is true of any other commodity, labour-power has a two-fold, or dialectical nature, viz., use-value and exchange-value. The exchange-value is the basis of the wage and is determined by the labour-time socially necessary for the production of workers' necessities, i.e., the value of these necessities. The use-value of labour-power is labour (p.283), and, here again, labour has the aforementioned two-fold, or dialectical, character. To recap, concrete labour is the particular skill or technique that produces the use-value of commodities. Abstract, or socially homogeneous, labour is measured by its duration; it is, therefore, the labour-time during which labour-power impregnates other commodities with value. As Marx explains, the value involved in maintaining labour-power and the value created by labour-power "...are two totally different things. The former determines the exchange-value of labour-power, the latter its use-value." (p. 300)

Because labour-power's use-value, i.e., labour, has a dialectical nature so too does the immediate process of capitalist production. At one and the same time, labour is used to create use-values and to create value; these simultaneous processes shape and determine one another, as do the opposites in any internal relation. The value creating process also has a dual, dialectical nature. Some of the labour-time that impregnates commodities with new value is necessary for producing the wage, but very essentially for capitalism, some of the labour-time is surplus to this necessary labour. This surplus labour creates surplus-value, which forms the basis of the capitalist's profits and thus capital itself. Although we tend to use the term capital rather loosely, technically it refers either to money invested in order to augment the value of the invested money or to any commodity bought for this purpose and used in its pursuit; importantly, however, its origin is the labour-capital relation—it is a form of value, like any form of value, that emerges within this relation. The amount of surplus-value produced depends on the ratio between necessary labour-time and surplus labour-time; in other words, the ratio between wages and surplus-value. This ratio is called the rate of surplus-value, or alternatively the rate of exploitation. For example, if the rate is 100%, it means that labourers work half of the time for themselves and the other half for the capitalist. The capitalist's goal is to increase the latter (the surplus) relative to the former (the necessary/wage).

The relational nature of the various elements depicted in Marx's explanation is not obvious to the participants in capitalist social relations. Moreover, certain elements, such as surplus-value, are not even visible. It is important to remember that Marx applied a scientific analysis to the observable phenomena, i.e., processes and results, in capitalist societies, and in this way he was operating in a similar manner to other scientists who use abstraction and exhaustive, logical, explanatory verification of their assertions. Having said this, it should not be surprising that capitalists are unaware of surplus-value or the rate of surplus-value; unless, of course, they have read Marx. Nevertheless, they manage to get their work force to produce surplus-value by constantly striving to increase their productivity. They know from experience that productivity is linked to their profitability. Increased productivity results in either maintaining or increasing profits depending on the degree of competition. They can achieve a goal they are unaware of, i.e., an increase in surplus-value, because every measure they take to increase productivity has the unobserved result of also increasing the surplus-value contained in the mass of commodities produced even when the necessary and surplus-value in each individual commodity is reduced. Further explanation of this aspect of productivity is given below.

There are two main methods by which surplus-value is produced and increased, both of which result in increased productivity. Marx calls the result of the first, and the original method, absolute surplus-value. This method of producing surplus-value involves extending the length of the working day beyond the period of time during which the value of the wage is created. Once the length of the working day is fixed by law, capitalists begin to utilise the second general method, which results in what Marx calls relative surplus-value. There are three ways of producing relative surplus-value, one of which is a derivative of the other two. Before explaining these, it is important to emphasise certain outcomes that occur when surplus-value is created, especially relative surplus-value. As mentioned previously, all these methods lead to an increase in labourers' productivity. With the advent of relative surplus-value, increased productivity means increasing the number of commodities produced in a given period of time, which, in turn, means that each commodity produced contains less newly created value, or less necessary/paid labour-time and less surplus/unpaid labour-time. It may appear illogical for capitalists to strive to cheapen their commodities; however, when they can produce, for example, two, three or four commodities in the same time during which they previously produced one commodity, the result will be more surplus-value. Capitalists focus on the profit they derive from the mass of commodities produced with a specific investment of capital, rather than the profit on each individual item. Another outcome, especially of relative surplus-value production, is that the consequent proliferation of commodities means capitalists must expand the demand for their commodities, in other words the expansion of the market. All the value, including the surplus-value, which is freshly created in the immediate process of production, is latent, or potential, value that is only realised when the commodity is sold.

Even though all the methods of creating relative surplus-value involve increasing productivity, it is only one of the methods that Marx refers to as increasing the "productivity of labour" (p. 655). This method entails producing commodities in less time or producing more commodities in "a given time with the same expenditure of labour" (p. 534). Marx refers to the second method of relative surplus-value production as the "intensification of labour" (p. 655). With this method more commodities are produced in a given length of time, with a greater expenditure of labour. To understand this second method, one needs to bear in mind that every hour, and therefore every labour hour as well as every socially necessary labour hour, is composed of 60 minutes. Therefore, the labour hour, for example, can be conceptualised as being more or less porous, i.e., more or less minutes of actual labour effort being expended (p. 534; Postone, 1996, p.292). The intensification of labour means a less porous, or more dense, labour hour. And when competition leads to this being generalised across all producers of a particular commodity, socially necessary labour-time will also reflect the less porous labour hour.

When either of the methods of extracting relative surplus-value takes hold in the firms that produce workers' necessities, the derivative method comes into play. The cost of the workers' necessities, necessities that are a socially and historically variable bundle of commodities and services, is reduced. As a consequence, the cost of labour-power will also be reduced. This decrease in the cost of labour-power leads to an increase in the rate of surplus-value for all capitalists because the ratio between paid and unpaid labour-time is increased in favour of the latter thus producing more relative surplus-value in the economy.

To completely understand why capitalists are so driven to increase their workers' productivity, we need to focus our attention on the market for one particular type of commodity. The socially necessary labour-time for the production of this commodity is reflected (objectified) in its market-value. It is important to note that exchange-value and market-value are the objectified forms of value around which prices, i.e., market-prices, fluctuate according to supply and demand. All of these elements arise from human beings' interactions with one another under the competitive conditions prevalent in past and present market transactions, but the only element that is visible to the participants is the market-price. The minimum requirement for each capitalist is to recoup the amount that they assume is the value of their commodity. They think that this amount derives from their constant capital, i.e., raw materials and equipment, the value of which is determined by past, or congealed, labour-time plus their variable capital, i.e., their workers' wages. Because they cannot see the surplus-value in their commodities and only see it in the form of profit when the commodity is sold, they think their profits come from exchange. They also think that their profits, i.e., the increase, which is over and above their investment, have been made possible by the total capital they have invested—the constant and the variable capital. Market-value, however, reflects both the socially necessary paid and the unpaid labour-time; therefore, capitalists who produce their commodities in less than the socially necessary labour-time can still sell their commodities for a price determined by market-value, or the socially necessary labour-time. Moreover, they can even sell at a lower price, and on the total mass of commodities produced in a given time, still maintain or even increase their profits, at least until their competitors adopt similar production techniques. What has happened behind the backs, so to speak, of all the producers of this commodity is that the surplus-value produced by the firms with the greatest number of workers, the ones producing the most latent surplus-value, pulls the market-value—an average—upwards, and this has the effect of redistributing the surplus-value produced by these firms to the firms with the smallest labour forces. Marx offers numerous examples of how this redistribution works with reference to the various forms of extorting relative surplus-value. For a synoptic version of these examples, see (Allman, 2001).

Even at this point in my précis of Marx's explanation, it is possible to discern some of the real anomalies in capitalism—anomalies that reflect the logically contradictory nature of this form of socio-economic organisation. First, if human needs and the overcoming of scarcity are placed at the forefront of our concerns, we can understand that capitalism's historically specific form of wealth is illogical to say nothing of unethical. Since wealth is based on value, human need for any use-value, which cannot be expressed in exchange-value, is denied, no matter how much it is needed or is essential to life. Moreover, it is only living labour that can create new value; constant capital only passes on in part or whole the value of past, or congealed, labour-time to each commodity produced. Nevertheless, capitalists, in striving to increase productivity, constantly reduce the newly expended labour-time in every commodity they produce. Therefore, they, unwittingly, strive to reduce the only source of the value-form of wealth. To make matters worse, their production decisions are always based primarily on the previous cycle of demand; and as a consequence, they can never know what level of productivity will glut the market and eventually lead to a crisis of overproduction. In a system based on the value-form of wealth, the only way to ameliorate this type of crisis is through devaluation, and devaluation means the destruction of commodities or their withdrawal from the market, e.g., the creation of surplus mountains often comprised of food commodities. Capitalism, thus, results in a cruel irony. It serves the progressive historical purpose of raising human productive capacities to a previously unimaginable level, one that could meet, at the very least, the basic needs of all human beings and thereby overcome scarcity. However, since the use-value of every commodity is internally related to its exchange-value, the human needs of a vast and growing number of the world's population are never met.

Thus far, the presentation of Marx's explanation has focussed on one of the two dialectical contradictions that constitute capital's essence, viz., the labour-capital relation of production—the relation within which surplus-value is produced. The entire capitalist production process, however, involves both the production of surplus-value and the realisation of surplus-value; therefore, the complete production process involves another internal relation, or dialectical contradiction, viz., the unity of the labour-capital relation, in the immediate process of production, with the processes of circulation and exchange. In one of the opposites of this unity, i.e., one of the opposites in dialectical contradiction two of capital's essence, surplus-value is created; in the other opposite, it is realised when the commodity is sold. When discussing capital's essence, I often include a third dialectical contradiction, viz., the internal relation between the social relations of production and the social forces of production. Superficially, this could be seen as simply another way of expressing the labour-capital relation; however, with a more comprehensive understanding of Marx's dialectical conceptualisation, one can interpret his use of this contradiction in a more complex manner. He refers to the relation between the social relations and social forces of production when trying to redirect attention to the way in which movements within capitalist production impact outward on the state and civil society and vice versa. In fact, Marx often beckons us to look at an internal relation, or dialectical contradiction, from another perspective by assigning it another name. Because the discussion of this relation involves consciousness and ideology, it is dealt with in Chapter 2.

When explaining capital at an introductory level, only a few additional comments are necessary about the processes of circulation and exchange. Capitalists always attempt to reduce circulation time. The more times capital can be turned-over during a given period, i.e., from the purchase of labour-power through the sale of the commodity, the more surplus-value, hence profit, will be realised by productive capitalists. Furthermore, the separation in time and space between the purchase of labour-power and the sale of the commodity leads to the possibility of dire imbalances in production. For example, in Volume 2 of *Capital* (1878:1978), Marx reveals the difficulty in striking a balance between the output of those firms that produce consumer goods and those that produce the capital goods, i.e., machinery and raw materials, needed by the producers of consumer goods. Given that output, or productivity, decisions are always estimated on the previous cycle of demand, from this circumstance alone, it can be seen that the potential for imbalances, or disparities, is enormous, often resulting in either over or underproduction. The longer the time between cycles of demand, the more precarious the situation.

The competitive race over circulation time as well as competition in general eventually lead to a division of labour amongst capitalists and, as a consequence, the division between those capitalists who only engage in production activities, i.e., the production of surplus-value, and those who engage solely in circulation and exchange, or commercial activities, i.e., the realisation of surplus-value. The use of credit also develops. Credit allows for a tremendous acceleration in the reproduction of capital. To cite but one example, credit enables the productive capitalists to recommence the immediate process of production prior to receiving their profits on the previous production cycle. With the development of the capitalist form of commercial capital (as opposed to the mercantile form that pre-dates capitalism) and the development of credit, not all the surplus-value realised from the sale of commodities returns to the productive capitalists for their use in further production. Some of it, of course, must always constitute the revenue, which capitalists use to purchase their own necessities and luxuries. However, as capitalism develops, value in its money form takes on many different functions, some of which lead to further divisions amongst capitalists and distinct forms of capital, e.g., financial capitalists and finance capital. Although the different functions and forms appear to be independent of one another, it is important to recognise that they are all claims on the surplus-value extorted by the productive capitalists from their labour forces. Marx's analytical power reaches its zenith in Volume 3 of *Capital* (1865:1981), where he provides exhaustive proof of this assertion. The assertion also brings us back, full circle, first to the labour-capital relation of production and then to the unity of that essential relation with circulation and exchange, or, in other words, to the essence of capital/capitalism.

Marx discovered the underlying essence of capital/capitalism by abstracting from the complex and very messy perplexity that characterises the concrete reality of a fully developed capitalist society—a reality wherein we find a multitude of capitals in competition with one another. This is the reality that Marx analyses in detail in the third volume of *Capital*. No longer does competition involve only the competition between sellers of the same commodity, or even the competitive struggle amongst firms in the same sphere of production. Importantly, and perhaps most crucially of all, it also involves competition amongst all capitalists for a finite amount of investment capital. It is this type of competition that leads to a tendency towards the equalisation of the rate of profit across all the various firms that constitute a capitalist economy.

In explaining the essence of capital, I mentioned that capitalists are unaware of the surplus-value their workers create and that they think the value of their commodity is constituted by its cost price, i.e., the sum of the constant capital used (machinery and raw materials) plus the variable capital (wages). That level of confusion would only have pertained to the early stages of capitalist development. One can only imagine the degree of confusion that results from fully developed capitalism, wherein market-value no longer directly reflects the average surplus-value produced in a particular branch or sphere of production but instead a general rate of profit that derives from the ratio between the mass of surplus-value produced across all the spheres of production and the total capital employed, i.e., the social capital. The development of the general rate of profit also means that the redistribution of surplus-value is taking place across all the firms in the economy. Although the value of constant and variable capital is still based on the socially necessary labour-time that is specific to a particular sphere of production, it is surplus-value that changes in form. It now reflects the general rate of profit, and thus derives from the total economy—the social capital—rather than any particular sphere. The commodity's market-value is, therefore, the sum of the commodity's cost price plus the product of the cost price multiplied by the general rate of profit, e.g., 20%. It is little wonder that capitalists are totally deluded by their observations of the surface reality of capitalism. When they sell their commodities, they receive neither the surplus-value contained in these commodities nor even the average surplus-value produced in their specific sphere of production. Instead, they receive a share of the total surplus-value produced in the economy, during a given period of time, according to the size of their capital investment. Fortunately, with Marx's penetrating scientific analysis of capital, it is possible to discover the essence, indeed the cause, of the concrete reality that shapes and determines so much of our contemporary human condition.

There are some extremely important and very real results of the unceasing drive to increase productivity that should be considered. These results are aspects of reality, which capitalists as well as many other observers of capitalism are incapable of comprehending. Marx explains these results by first drawing our attention to the value composition of various capitalist firms. He calls this value composition the organic composition. Once again, this is a relation, and in this case, it is the relation between the value of the constant capital as opposed to the value of the variable capital. Capitals with a high organic composition have relatively more value invested in constant than variable capital; therefore, they tend to be much more productive than firms with a lower organic composition, i.e., labour-intensive firms. Moreover, capitals with the highest organic composition in their sphere of production produce a higher rate of profit on their total investment of capital. Their enhanced labour productivity means they can produce, for example, three commodities in the same amount of time during which their competitors produce one. Moreover, even though their costs, i.e., the sum of the constant and variable capital, and the surplus-value produced are spread over three rather than one item, thus making each item much cheaper, they can continue to charge the same price as their competitors, a price determined by the market-value. In this case they obtain super-profits. Of course, they can only do this for as long as the market-value of their commodity is sustained by the competitive participation of more labour-intensive firms, i.e., firms with a lower organic composition. In other words, the advantage gained by having a relatively higher organic composition than the average for a particular sphere can be very short-lived. Higher organic composition actually reduces the amount of surplus-value produced and the rate of profit. Nevertheless, the firm that adopts the higher composition first, before the mean composition alters due to similar changes by the original firm's competitors, wins the previously mentioned short-term advantage. Furthermore, as a result of its higher profit rate on the capital invested, the firm with the highest organic composition attracts more investment capital, at least until competitors catch up by changing the organic composition of their capital investments. To reiterate, it is this flow of investment capital into and out of firms according to rising or lowering profit rates that creates the tendency towards the formation of a general rate of profit and which alters the form in which surplus-value appears in the constitution of the commodity's value and also, as already noted, its market-value. Marx signals this transformation of surplus-value into the general rate of profit by referring to commodity-value in the same terms used by the bourgeois economist David Ricardo; hence, commodity-values are transformed into prices of production. Prices of production reflect the appearance of surplus-value on the surface of capitalist society; in other words, the concrete appearance from which Marx began his analysis.

Competition for investment capital encourages capitalists to change the organic composition of their capital investment, thus constantly moving towards a high enough organic composition to remain competitive. However, since it is only living labour that can create new value, the overall result of all of this movement is to produce a tendency for the general rate of profit to fall. Marx calls this result "The Law of the Tendential Fall in the Rate of Profit" (Marx, 1865:1981, p. 318). Besides discussing in detail how this law comes into existence with the full development of capitalism, Marx also discusses several factors that can counter, or more precisely, attenuate the falling rate of profit. It is important to emphasise that these counteracting factors only slow or temporarily halt the fall in the rate of profit; they are temporary counters to the operation of the law. The law itself, however, will be constantly reasserted. Here, I cite only a few examples of these counteracting factors, but first it is important to consider another fundamental outcome of the drive to increase productivity and the resulting move towards capitals of higher organic composition. This result, like the fall in the general rate of profit, is problematic for the capitalists, but the real calamity for all of humanity is that it suggests that environmental destruction, or at the very least severe abuse, is an inherent feature of capitalism.

Capitalists cannot help but be aware of the fall in the general rate of profit, but it is not a grave concern to them if they can maintain or preferably increase the mass of profits they appropriate. What we have just seen in terms of the entire economy suffering a falling rate of profit because of the higher average organic composition of the social capital, actually takes place first with changes in the organic composition of individual firms and eventually the spheres of production in which they operate. Whenever there is a decline in the rate of profit at any of these levels, capital accumulation is the only way to prevent a decline in the mass of profits. Growth in the size and concentration of capital, in fact, comes to characterise a fully developed capitalist economy. Here is how it works on the level of the individual capitalist firm. To simply maintain their profits, when there is a fall in the rate of profit, capitalists must increase the size of their capital investment. For example, if the profits on a capital investment of 1 million fall from 400,000 to 200,000 because of a drop in the profit rate from 40% to 20%, then profits of 400,000 can only be maintained if the capital investment is doubled, i.e., increased to 2 million (20% of 2 million = 400,000). If capitalists wish to increase their profits, the accumulation, or increase in investment, must be even greater. For example, to raise these profits to 440,000, an increase of 40, 000, an investment of 2, 220, 000, a rise of 220%, would be needed (20% of 2,220,000 = 440,000). (pp. 328-329) It perhaps goes without saying, that this type of unplanned growth, across the economy, has had and will continue to have dreadful effects on the environment, and this is the reason for the earlier assertion that environmental destruction/abuse is an inherent feature of capitalism.

As mentioned above, Marx details several counteracting factors that can attenuate the fall in the general rate of profit. With some of these counteracting factors, we come face to face, once again, with the logically contradictory nature of capitalism. As Marx puts it, "...the same factors that produce the tendency for the rate of profit to fall also moderate the realization of this tendency." (p. 343) For example, the machinery that increases the value of constant capital relative to variable capital also increases the intensity of labour thus raising the rate of surplus-value. As mentioned earlier, the rate of surplus-value is the ratio of paid to unpaid labour, i.e., variable capital to surplus-value. At a rate of 100%, workers work half of the time for themselves, reproducing their wages, and the other half for the capitalist, thus passing on the same value in paid and unpaid labour to each commodity. However, at a more intense rate, e.g., 110%, relatively more surplus-value is passed on to each commodity, thereby slowing down, and even sometimes temporarily halting, the falling rate of profit.

Another example of what Marx means can be seen in the counteracting effect brought about by the cheapening of the elements of constant capital. To reiterate, competition promotes the capitalists' drive to increase productivity, which brings about the move towards higher organic composition and the consequent fall in the rate of profit. However, when the firms that produce the various elements of constant capital become more productive, the value of their output is cheapened just as it would be with any commodity. Therefore, the mass of constant capital can grow more quickly than its value relative to variable capital. When the value of constant capital relative to variable capital decreases, the falling rate of profit is attenuated. Foreign trade involving the importation of cheaper constant capital produces the same result. Remember that the organic composition is the value composition of the capital not the technical composition. In other words, two firms might have the same technical composition, the same amount of constant capital, but the value composition of one of them can be higher or lower than the other.

Of course, foreign trade can also cheapen the cost of workers' necessities, thus lowering the price of labour-power, or in other words, the value of variable capital. However, this also brings about a rise in the rate of surplus-value, which as just explained, slows the fall in the rate of profit. Also with respect to foreign trade, firms that sell their commodities in foreign markets where the mean organic composition is lower reap super-profits in the same way that the domestic firm that first moves to a higher organic composition does at home. Finally, firms can move their production, or outsource some portion of it, abroad in order to secure a lower cost price. As long as the firm retains its base in its country of origin, its profits will figure in the equalisation of the rate of profit in the home nation, thus stemming the fall in the general rate of profit. Moreover, if such activity comes to characterise a major part of a nation's economic activity, it can even temporarily reverse the fall in the general rate of profit. The capitalist economy that does this will have simply displaced its contradictions (Harvey, 1999), for the time being, moving them to the global arena where they become even more complex and, when the law is eventually reasserted, more disastrous for humanity.

With these and several other examples of counteracting factors, Marx's explanation of the law of the falling rate of profit not only reveals why and how it comes into existence but also, and importantly, why the general rate of profit doesn't fall faster, thereby making the law operate more as a tendency than an unremitting law.

This very brief but relatively comprehensive précis of *Capital* Volumes 1-3, Marx's brilliant 'outing' of capital's essence as well as the manifestation of this essence in the concrete reality of fully developed capitalist societies, should enable a brief consideration of capitalism's culpability in some of the major problems currently facing humanity. The four problems selected are some of the most portentous aspects of the contemporary human condition. In many ways, not least of all capitalism itself, they are all interconnected. I begin with credit and debt and then go on to consider globalisation, environmental destruction and poverty.

MARX'S PURCHASE ON 21ST CENTURY PROBLEMS

Credit & Debt

When the money form of value, i.e., some amount of it, spins off from its original functions of circulating commodities and acting as a means of payment for them, one result is the development of finance capital. This is the most mystified and fetishised form of capital because its source, as a share of the surplus-value derived from productive capital, is totally obscured. On the surface of capitalist reality, it actually appears that a certain sum of money, without any commodity intervening, can simply create an augmented value. Money is lent to the productive capitalists, at a pre-determined rate of interest, and the rate of interest on the money advanced together with the original sum advanced is returned to the money-lender. The rate of interest, which actually bears no relation to the production of surplus-value, is determined by the supply and demand for money. Usury, or money-lending for profit, pre-dates capitalism and is one of the pre-conditions for the advent of capitalism; however, as capitalism develops and the division of labour amongst capitalists takes place, finance capital emerges as a new, more complex and sophisticated form of usury. In modern capitalism, finance capitalists deal in a variety of commodities, including derivatives and futures, but for this discussion the focus is on money-lending and thus the commodities referred to as loans and credit.

Money-lending capitalists cannot depend solely on selling their loans or credit to productive capitalists because the need for investment in production goes through cycles. For example, whenever there is overproduction, the demand for investment dries up, and if there were no other consumers of loans and credit, this would move the interest rate to zero and force the money-lending capitalists out of business. Therefore the financial capitalists who deal in loans and credit must create additional demand. It is important to realise that credit is actually immanent in capitalism. If for no other reason, this would be the case simply because of the separation in time and space between the purchase of labour-power and the sale of commodities. The demand for credit and loans develops at a rapid pace with the development of capitalism. In fact, the demand has grown so extensively that finance capital increasingly appears to have no relation whatsoever with the production of surplus-value. Establishing the connection is beyond the scope of this text (see Marx, *Capital*, Vol. 3 for the connection); nevertheless, with this preliminary background, it is now possible to consider, in some degree of depth, the calamity commonly known as 'The Third World Debt Crisis'. At least some of the points raised may ring alarm bells with regard to consumer credit, that seemingly irresistible little commodity that increasing numbers of people are using to supplement their actual incomes.

To understand the contemporary debt crisis that plagues many under-developed and developing countries, we need to start with capitalism in the 1930's. During that decade, capitalism suffered its most severe crisis ever of overproduction, the onset of which was signalled with the famous American Stock Market crash of 1929. With an abundance of commodities remaining unsold, the latent surplus-value they contained completely lost value resulting in a spate of bankruptcies throughout the US economy. Of course, the failure of the US economy had a knock-on effect elsewhere until many of the nations of the capitalist world were suffering depression, recession or at the very least an economic downturn. Nevertheless, for the capitalist system as a whole this was a propitious situation because the devaluation it entailed served to partially cleanse the system of its overproduction. The devastation wreaked by World War II, especially in Europe, completed the cleansing as devaluation reached unprecedented levels. In effect, this massive devaluation prepared the way for a period of renewed accumulation, in fact, the most extensive period of capitalist growth to date. This period has been hailed as capital's 'Golden Age'.

By the 1970's, however, signs of stagnation began to reappear. The surplus-population, i.e., the unemployed, increased, as did surplus-capital, i.e., capital that could not be profitably invested in an already saturated production process. Then in 1974, this situation was seriously exacerbated when the cartel of oil producing nations raised the price of oil. The excess profits that flowed from this move created an even greater amount of surplus capital, i.e., loan capital in excess of the existing market demand for loans. Clearly, new sources of demand had to be found or created. It should come as no surprise that quite suddenly loans became one of the hottest commodities on the world market. Intense competition to find profitable outlets for the surplus-capital meant that loans were offered to under-developed and lesser-developed countries at irresistibly low rates. At that time, the sages of development theory and policy were in agreement that this influx of money was exactly what these countries needed to get on the development bandwagon. Despite considerable evidence to the contrary, capitalists in the developed world, then as well as now, peddle the belief that there is room for everyone in the capitalist club. They ignore the zero-sum nature of capitalism, a system which inherently requires winners and losers and thus in both national and international economies uneven levels of development.

The vast majority of the loans sold during the 1970's were commercial rather than governmental loans, but by the 1980's, two events in particular had led the commercial lenders to become much more cautious. In 1982, the Mexican government defaulted on its loans. Shortly after this major shock, the US government launched its 'Star Wars' programme. Accordingly, US defence spending soared, and, to everyone's amazement, the United States became the world's largest debtor (George, 1988). The result of this new increased demand for loans was that interest rates spiralled upwards, plunging the 'Third World' debtor nations into the now familiar debt crisis. One can argue that it was people's irrational belief in the progressive nature of capitalist development that was the real culprit in this crisis. However, as discussed in Chapter 2, since it is people's experience of capital's contradictions that produces the distorted understanding of capitalism, it is more convincing to argue that it is capitalism, itself, that is responsible for the 'Third World' debt crisis. Needless to say, since the majority of loans are commercial, the new found morality that encourages Western governments to 'forgive' these debts can do little more than ease some of the most devastating effects of the crisis. Given the level of suffering in these nations, such forgiving must be supported but not accompanied by the hopeful yet uncritical notion that the crisis will go away.

Globalisation

The capitalists' quest to produce and realise value, especially surplus-value, and to find the most propitious conditions for accomplishing their goal propels capital all over the world, establishing capitalism as a global socio-economic system. This is a system with an ever-expanding global market in commodified goods, services and also capital, itself, in its real commodity and money forms as well as its various fictitious forms, which are no more than claims on future production. Globalisation, like credit, is yet another immanent feature of capitalism. If globalisation appears to be a new phenomenon, it is due to the unprecedented growth in the universalisation of capitalism that has occurred during the last thirty years (Wood, 1995, 1999). The process of globalisation, at least on planet earth, will never cease until every object of human need is commodified and every human being who must sell his or her labour to earn a living has been subsumed within the labour-capital relation. Moreover, since human beings are not likely to stop reproducing the species and human needs are not likely to stop expanding, the only possible terminus to the capitalist process of globalisation is the demise of capitalism.

The most recent onslaught of globalisation seems more pervasive than ever not just because of its extent but also because of the speed at which value in its various forms moves around the world, accelerated by enormous developments in telecommunication. In the contemporary world of capitalism, value, in its real and fictitious forms, changes hands with the speed of light thus producing, in effect, the compression of time and space (Harvey, 1989). However, technological developments did not cause the contemporary thrust of capital throughout the globe. This phase, as is true of any phase, of globalisation is the result of the unremitting drive, indeed necessity, to locate new outlets for the temporary resolution of capitalism's inherent contradictions. To understand more complexly this most recent phase of globalisation, it is important to consider the significant historical conditions that provoked it.

During the post World War II 'Golden Age' of capitalism, productivity, profits and wages grew in concert. It even appeared that the progressive development of capitalism had made the labour-capital relation more harmonious. Of course, it could only appear this way if one forgot the trade union struggles for better wages and conditions, which produced this degree of harmony. Appearances aside, labour in the developed capitalist world was stronger than it previously had been, and it was widely assumed on both sides of the labour-capital relation that agreed increases in productivity would be linked to wage rises. The post World War II welfare state, in whatever degree it was instituted in various capitalist nations, bolstered people's belief in progress, lulling working people into what turned out to be a false sense of security and increasing strength. In the 1970's, when stagnation reappeared, the inherent logic of the capitalist system made it clear to many capitalists as well as the national governments that supported them that adjustments not just in the economy but also in social attitudes were drastically required.

As many capitalist firms moved into the global arena, unfettering themselves from their over-accumulated and concentrated national bases and their expectation-rich workforces, a new philosophy of capitalist progress came into play, rapidly developing into an ideology that eventually would invade nearly every aspect of people's existence in the developed capitalist world. The mantras of neo-liberalism have become so pervasive that this ideology no longer needs an introduction. Liberalism, the philosophy from which it springs, is, of course, hardly new and traces back at least to Adam Smith's advocacy of free markets. In ideological terms, however, neo-liberalism is distinctive in the extent to which it has penetrated people's consciousness, changing the way people understand and feel about their existence in capitalist societies. In some subtle and some not so subtle ways, the meanings attributed to several of our most fundamental concepts have changed. For example, in democratic societies, the concept 'freedom' has long been linked to certain enshrined unalienable rights, but during capital's 'Golden Age', it also became linked to other progressive notions such as freedom from oppression, unemployment and want. The proponents of neo-liberalism have managed to break the link between freedom and these progressive notions and to link freedom instead to the market friendly notion of choice. As a result, we are free so long as we can choose from the options capitalism has on offer. In fact, the rhetoric of the present US executive branch, which refers to freedom ad nauseam, seems to use freedom as a synonym not just for market choice but also for capitalism, itself. Freedom is one small but very important example of how the ideology of neo-liberalism has been working, since the 1980's, to change social attitudes and to prepare the ground for renewed capitalist profitability and growth through the necessary and unrelenting processes of globalisation (Harvey, 2005).

The only way that neo-liberalism, or any other ideology, can gain this degree of persuasive strength is by effectively enabling people to make some sense of what they are actually experiencing in capitalist societies. As noted previously, the stagnation of the 1970's made many supporters of capitalism realise that capitalism was suffering from a deficiency in an essential ingredient. Competition, although never entirely absent in capitalist economies, had become sluggish; therefore, the required antidote was free trade, especially the liberalisation of markets and the removal of any barriers to the movement of value. It is an unfortunate irony for capitalism that so few capitalists have read Marx. He explained well over a century ago why competition was necessary for the proper functioning of the laws of capitalism, thus essential to its normal functioning (see especially Marx, 1865: 1981). When the need for renewing competitive conditions finally dawned on capital's proponents, the process of globalisation was given new impetus. Heavily accumulated and concentrated national residues of capital were broken up and moved to new locations around the world where they could be managed more flexibly and where more profitable conditions could be found. It goes without saying that one of these more profitable conditions was new sources of labour-power that were not satiated with feelings of strength and rich in expectations. The new more profitable conditions that could be found in the global arena were the immediate 'fix' that capitalism required.

The globalisation of capital has never been nor will it ever be an unidirectional process, i.e., the migration of capital from its home nation. To reiterate, by seeking out new production bases throughout the globe, many capitalists were able to produce commodities more profitably, i.e., the commodities contained more latent, or potential, surplus-value; however, this potential surplus-value also must be realised through the sale of commodities for the increased profitability to become a reality. As a consequence, capitalists never lose sight of effective demand, and to date the consumer market that can express, with money, the greatest demand remains in the developed world. Therefore, once labour in various regions of the developed world has been effectively disciplined, e.g., has become more 'flexible' regarding pay, conditions and expectations, capital, or at least some portion of it, can safely and profitably move back to its country of origin where it gains the additional advantage of proximity to the consumers who can most effectively express demand. The story, of course, doesn't end here. It begins all over again, but this time capitalist growth, i.e., accumulation and concentration, takes place in a more complex and perplexing global arena.

Due to the introductory nature of this text, the discussion of globalisation has sketched only the bare details of the ongoing processes of globalisation, i.e., some of what has happened to date and some of what can be expected in the future. The intention is that this discussion might serve as a guide for further research and that it might lay the foundations for a critical understanding of globalisation, one that is strong enough to enable readers to challenge the current 'political wisdom', which alleges that globalisation is an inevitable historical development, a force of history much like a force of nature, that lies beyond human control and thus beyond the horizon of democratic choice and decision making. Globalisation is no more inevitable than the capitalist socio-economic system that produces it.

Environmental Destruction

At a time when most of his contemporary intellectuals were enthralled by the possibility of humanity gaining control over nature, Marx's prescience led him to a much more informed scepticism. He warned his contemporaries that "...the theoretical discovery of [nature's] laws appears merely as a ruse to subjugate it..." (Marx, 1858:1973, p.410). He also argued that capitalists' unplanned, uncoordinated and irrational drive to increase productivity was bound to have a detrimental affect on the natural world. For example, with reference to capitalist production in agriculture, he warned: "Capitalist production...only develops the...social processes of production by simultaneously undermining the original sources of all wealth—the soil and the worker." (Marx, 1867: 1976, p. 638) He went on to explain that, in the long term, capitalist production would deplete the fertility and nutritional quality of the soil, and this, in turn, would have disastrous consequence for people's health.

Although Marx acknowledged capitalism's role in developing the productive capabilities of human beings and its role in enriching human needs to an unprecedented degree, he warned that it was doing this in a way that was sowing the seeds for environmental destruction. He would have abhorred the development policies pursued in the former Soviet Union and in China. According to Marx's vision of socialism/communism (see Allman, 1999), human productivity would have to be developed in concert with environmental health. He considered humanity and the environment to be an internally related unity of opposites; therefore, if either opposite were to develop in a manner that was detrimental to the other, the internal relation would become an inherently antagonistic dialectical contradiction, which over time would lead to the abolition of both opposites.

To my knowledge, with but a few exceptions, (e.g., Burkett, 1999; Liodakis, 2001; Harvey, 1995), the environmental movement has yet to produce someone who can conceptualise environmental problems within a philosophy, or concept, of internal relations. Even the most well informed prognoses regarding the health of the planet issue from a framework of assumptions that arise from capitalist social relations, i.e., assumptions framed totally within capitalism's horizon of debate (Hall, 1982). For example, many critics of environmental destruction claim that the only way to save the planet is to put the brakes on economic growth. When 'growth' is assumed entirely on a capitalist basis and when the vast majority of the world's population has not benefited at all from capitalist driven growth, such claims may not be just misguided but also unethical.

The idea that human beings, with the aid of scientific and technological innovations, can gain sufficient control of the environment to stop and maybe even reverse environmental degradation still persists. The most obvious example of its persistence is the US executive branch refusal, until quite recently, to even acknowledge the existence of global warming. The recent turn-around is highly suspicious. It is more likely a highly compromised, condescending, acceptance of the problem in the face of overwhelming evidence, backed by mounting pressure from concerned US citizens and foreign allies of the US. If this is the case, then it is certain that any measures taken to address the problem of global warming will be equally compromised. Even if the US leadership were to actually take the problem seriously, any solutions proposed would be framed within parameters defined by capitalism. Marx would have argued that capitalist health and environmental health are not compatible because within capitalist social relations, society's relation with nature is necessarily antagonistic, i.e., nature must be controlled and dominated by human beings, or more precisely capital.

Poverty

Whether we click our fingers every three minutes to indicate a child dying due to poverty, as in a recent TV commercial, or cite Oxfam's current estimate of 50, 000 dying daily from poverty, the statistics are appalling; living in poverty is worse than appalling and allowing others to do so is inexcusable. Poverty is indisputably the greatest scandal of the 21st Century. The continuing existence, and even growth, of poverty in this period of humanity's history when human beings' productive capacities could overcome most forms of scarcity is a condition historically specific to capitalism. When Marx's explanation of capitalism is taken in its entirety, it is possible to understand why poverty is immanent in capitalism. This brief discussion of poverty begins with capitalism's utmost obstacle to the eradication of poverty, viz., the capitalist form of wealth.

As mentioned previously, the value-form of wealth is historically specific to capitalism. The capitalists' drive to create profits (surplus-value) raises human productivity to an unprecedented level, the result of which is a great mass of commodities. Every commodity, be it a tangible item or a service, is a unity of use-value and exchange-value. However, capitalist wealth is based exclusively on exchange-value; therefore, use-values, for which there is either no or insufficient demand expressed in money or credit, are either destroyed or removed from the market. Furthermore, in the world of global capitalism, there is another option that is equally disastrous. Sometimes, the unsold commodities are 'dumped' in foreign markets, i.e., sold very cheaply. As a result local producers are undercut and soon driven out of business and into either poverty or the market for labour-power. Capitalists will 'dump' even when they can't initially recoup a profit because the 'dumping' gives them access to the foreign markets that promise to become very lucrative once the local competition is eliminated. The value form of wealth is one of the greatest absurdities of capitalism. Moreover, since it is the pursuit of only this form of wealth that counts, the suitability and quality of the use-values produced are often not conducive to either human beings or the environment.

The world of global capitalism is plagued by uneven development; and many individuals and organisations devote all their energies to closing the developmental gap. However, Marx's explanation of capitalism suggests why uneven levels of socio-economic development both between and within nations is not only propitious for capital but absolutely necessary. As discussed previously, the relentless drive to increase productivity leads, in turn, to the emergence of firms with a higher organic composition of capital, i.e., firms with increasingly more value invested in constant capital than variable capital (labour-power). With reference to a particular sphere of production, the move to higher organic composition is only profitable when there are other firms with a lower organic composition producing the same commodity, i.e., less developed firms. If this were not the case, the redistribution of surplus-value from the firms of low organic composition to those of high organic composition could not take place. To reiterate, the firms with relatively more labour serve to pull the market-value of this commodity upwards, and since the firm/firms with high organic composition can still sell their commodities for the market-value even when the value of their commodities is much less, the result is that surplus-value is in effect redistributed to the firms whose commodities contain the least surplus-value. The multinational and transnational corporations can actually achieve this redistribution of surplus-value internally by having some components of a commodity or even some of the commodities manufactured by the corporation produced in countries where a lower organic composition of capital, i.e., labour-intensive production, still prevails. The need to maintain uneven levels of national development, despite all the rhetoric to the contrary, is one of the greatest ironies as well as one of the greatest hypocrisies of capitalism. Capitalism will always require firms, regions and nations that use labour-intensive production processes simply because capitalism's historically specific form of wealth, the value-form, can only be created by living labour.

Finally, one of the most insidious outcomes of capitalism is that an ever-increasing number of the world's population is becoming surplus to capital's requirements. Capitalists will always try to expand the global reach of their markets and to locate new cheap sources of labour-power, but with the growing disparities between the rich and the poor, there are simply some regions of the world and even some locations within the developed nations that show no potential for participation in the market. Rather than helping to develop these areas, capitalists find it more profitable to expend their efforts on making already effective consumers more and more needy. Just how the capitalist world is going to deal with the consequences of this surplus population is a serious question for every citizen of the globe, indeed, a serious question for the very meaning and substance of humanity, itself.

Each of the problems addressed in this section is being challenged by groups and individuals throughout the world. With but few exceptions, the resulting campaigns, demonstrations and movements focus on reforming some aspect or another of capitalism. Greedy individual capitalists, unfair trade, unaware citizens and uncaring governments are frequently identified as the 'enemy' in need of reform or outright prohibition. Given the dismal results of these four problems and many others, the need for reform is undeniable. However, since, as Marx tried so diligently to explain, the real 'enemy' is capitalism, it is important to be critically aware of the limitations to reform. In either the medium or the long term, reforms contribute to the falling rate of profit and the attenuation of competition both of which lead to economic stagnation or even crisis and thus, ultimately, the reversal of the reforms. Reforms buy time but little more. Following Marx, it is crucial to recognise that even something as insidious as capitalists' greed does not spring from an asocial personality trait but rather arises as a necessary consequence of individuals operating according to a logic that is dictated by the inherent laws of capital. Needless to say, these seemingly intractable problems will remain predominant features of contemporary reality until a sufficient number of people develop a critical understanding of capitalism and then begin to name and challenge the real enemy.

CHAPTER 1 SUMMARY

Most of the chapter is devoted to a fairly comprehensive but highly condensed précis of Marx's exposition of his critical analysis of capital/capitalism, i.e., Volumes 1-3 of Marx's *Capital*. The chapter is based on the assumption that readers have read and understood, to some degree, the description of Marx's dialectical conceptualisation, i.e., the critical orientation and conceptual tools that constitute his analytical approach and that are explained in the Introduction to this text. The précis is followed by a concise discussion of four problems of considerable consequence in contemporary capitalism: credit and debt, globalisation, environmental destruction and poverty. Certain aspects of Marx's explanation of capitalism are applied in considering each of these problems and in order to suggest how readers might begin to develop a more critical understanding of capital's culpability in the creation and maintenance of the problem.

CHAPTER 1 QUESTIONS

1) Select another social and/or economic problem. If your thinking were to be totally confined within capitalism's 'horizon of debate', what questions would you ask; what reasons would you offer to explain the problem and what solution/s would you suggest?

2) With reference to the problem you selected for question 1), what questions, reasons and solutions would be suggested by Marx's critical analysis of capital/capitalism?

3) When considering any or all of the following, how would a concept of internal relations influence your understanding: love/marriage; human beings and the environment; civil society and the state.

MARX ON CONSCIOUSNESS

Marx's enormous intellectual project and political activism were driven and sustained by a motivation far more profound than scholarly curiosity. He had an abiding belief in the possibility of human beings and also humanity becoming more than they were at any one point in history. For Marx, to be fully human, human beings, meant that people would be continuously engaged in a process of becoming, a process of developing all of their potentials (Marx, 1844a:1972; 1858: 1973). Of course, Marx understood that the realisation of this latent potentiality depended upon human beings' collective engagement in self and social transformation. His critical utopian vision together with his understanding of the prerequisites for achieving it were almost certainly the main factors that motivated him to discover the laws of capitalism—thus producing for humanity at least the intellectual weapons that would be needed for a transformational struggle against capital. Marx began his economic studies in the early 1840's, but it was not until the late 1850's that he was in a position that would allow him to devote his full intellectual energies to discovering and then communicating the laws of capitalism. However, ten years before he undertook this endeavour, he produced a unique and equally important theory of consciousness. In 1846, Marx, in collaboration with Engels, completed *The German Ideology*, the text in which this theory of consciousness was first expressed. Unfortunately, this important work was not published until 1932, despite the best efforts of the authors. Nevertheless, the basic tenets of the theory together with its further elaboration are integral to Marx's economic writings. In fact, Marx's theory of consciousness explains why the laws of capital can only be discovered by means of a critical scientific analysis. It is also a theory with enormous implications for education, implications that are considered in the next chapter. First, however, it is important to explain the theory and to discuss the general implications and logical extensions pertaining to it.

THE THEORY, ITS LOGICAL EXTENSIONS & IMPLICATIONS

Quite often, Marx presents his ideas in the form of a critique, and his original presentation of his theory of consciousness was no exception. In other words, he presents his theory through a critique of other people's thinking, i.e., the general form of their thinking as well as, in this case, their understanding of consciousness, especially the origin of consciousness. When Marx and Engels wrote *The German Ideology*, there were two predominant theories of the origin of consciousness. Idealism, one of these theories, and the one with the longest historical legacy, holds that ideas, or consciousness, are antecedent to the material (real) world. In other words, the real world is the result of consciousness. The other theory, which is a form of materialism, a mechanical and unhistorical form, proposes the exact opposite; ideas and consciousness are the result of sensory projections of material phenomena. Marx was critical of the dichotomised type of thinking that underpinned both of these theories. In each case the real world (material world) and consciousness are conceptualised as separate and distinct entities/phenomena. There also is no reciprocity between material reality and consciousness; all movement between the two takes place in only one direction. These two theories differ only in so far as the entity to which causal significance, and thus movement, is attributed. Marx was critical not just of how dichotomised thinking produced these theories but also of how the dichotomising of reality and consciousness encouraged reified, and in its worse form fetishised, thought (both of which are discussed later in this chapter).

In contrast and critical opposition to these theories, Marx formulated an inimitable and revolutionary theory of consciousness that permitted no dichotomy, or binary separation, between consciousness and reality. As readers may already have anticipated, Marx conceptualises consciousness and reality as an internally related unity of opposites. Additionally, reality is conceptualised dynamically, as the sensuous, active experience of human beings in the material world. Therefore, at any one moment in time, consciousness is comprised of thoughts that arise from each human being's sensuous activity. Moreover, the consciousness of any human being will also include thoughts that have arisen external to the individual's own sensuous activity, i.e., from other people's sensuous activity both historically and contemporaneously. However, individuals' only integrate these external sources of consciousness through actively engaging with them. Since Marx's theory of consciousness posits the dialectical unity of human thought and practice, it is actually a theory of praxis but more, much more, on this later. To reiterate, according to Marx, thinking and action, consciousness and sensuous human experience, are inseparable. Marx's theory also proposes that the sensuous activity that has the greatest impact on consciousness is people's experience within the social relations in which they engage in order to produce their material world, i.e., their experience within historically specific social relations of production— relations that determine both how they produce and what they produce (1846:1976, p. 37).

When taken together with his critical analysis of capitalism, Marx's theory of consciousness leads to several other significant insights. To begin with, because human beings' sensuous activity takes place within historically specific social relations, e.g., capitalist social relations of production, the general characteristics of consciousness are also historically specific. In other words, the consciousness of people living within capitalist social relations will have general characteristics that are different from the characteristics of consciousness that prevailed, for example, in feudal societies and thus feudal social relations.

Although Marx does not specifically refer to the constitution of human subjectivity, his theory of consciousness implies that people's feelings, their subjectivities, are constituted in the same manner as their consciousness. When people sensuously engage with the material world, their thoughts and feelings, their objective and subjective responses, are produced simultaneously. Therefore, Marx's theory of consciousness involves not only the dialectical, or internal, relation between consciousness and material practice but also, by logical extension, an internal relation between human objectivity and subjectivity.

Clearly, Marx's theory of consciousness entails conceptualising according to internal relations. Thinking in terms of internal relations in general and in terms of Marx's theory of consciousness in particular can be difficult to express in human language, and this suggests yet another important insight that has to do with the limitations of human language. According to Marx, a great deal of human beings' sensuous experience within material reality, involves engagements within internal relations or engagements with one or the other of the components of an internal relation. Prior to the acquisition of language, very young children, who tend to think through their actions, or externally, find it natural to encounter a world of relations. Because the internalisation of thought is a developmental process that takes place during early childhood, it is possible to observe an external form of thought as it is expressed in the child's action concepts (Allman, 2001). In these action concepts, the relational nature of sensuous experience can be expressed and thus observed; however, once thought is fully internalised, it is normally expressed in language, which develops in concert with the internalisation of thought. Herein lies the problem, or rather part of the problem—language expresses concepts that tend to obscure, even extinguish, the relational origin of these concepts. With the continuing development of language throughout life, this problem could confound our ability to think in terms of internal relations to say nothing of our ability to express such thinking; unless, of course, we remain vigilant and critically aware of the inherent limitations in even one of the most prized abilities of the human species. Marx, however, did not assign primary culpability to language. The source of the distortions was a material world of commodity production wherein the components of the relations not only appear to exist independently but in some cases also develop an independent existence and are experienced as such and also where some of these relations are only experienced in objectified forms that also obscure their relational origin (e.g. Marx, 1858: 1973, p.164; 1867:1976, p. 177). Therefore, language only expresses distortions already present in reality. Nevertheless, even when Marx's science enables us to recognise the relational nature of our material world, the language conventions and concepts, which have developed from human practice in historically specific ways during capitalist history, can make it more difficult to express the true nature of reality, including, of course, one's own and others' experiences.

Earlier, I briefly asserted that Marx's theory of consciousness was actually a theory of praxis, i.e., a theory of the inseparable unity of thought and practice rather than a sequential theory of praxis (a thought-action-thought-action-etc. sequence). For me, this is the most crucial insight that can be drawn from Marx's theory of consciousness because if that theory is considered together with Marx's critical analysis of capitalism, logic suggests that it can only mean that human praxis has the potential to exist in two very different and opposed forms (see also Kosík, 1976). If people only engage in the social relations, into which they are born, assuming all the while that these relations, or practices, are natural and inevitable, then their praxis (the unity of their thought and action) will be uncritical and will serve only to reproduce the extant relations and conditions. Even people who operate at the forefront, or 'cutting-edge', of movements and developments within the given social relations and conditions, remain trapped within the horizon of capitalism. Since these movements and developments, in all likelihood, pertain to some accommodation or other, some temporary resolution or other, of capital's contradictions, the praxis of these 'progressives' actually supports and facilitates the necessary developments and as a consequence the reproduction of capitalist social relations as well as the given conditions of humanity's existence.

Alternatively, people can choose to critically question the existing social relations and to engage in transforming, or abolishing, them whilst also developing new social relations and conditions aimed at creating a better existence for all human beings. When people make this choice, they are choosing what I call critical/revolutionary praxis rather than and in opposition to uncritical/reproductive praxis (Allman, 1999; 2001). Marx's explanation of capitalism, his theory of consciousness (praxis) and the possibility of critical/revolutionary praxis, when taken together, strongly suggest that authentic revolution requires the simultaneous and complementary transformation of both self and society. Neither critical/revolutionary praxis nor authentic revolution can be imposed on people; both must be chosen on the basis of a critical understanding of capitalism and a deeply integrated desire to begin the process of shaping our own and thus humanity's future, or as Antonio Gramsci so aptly put it, on the basis of "...the intellectual base [being] so well rooted, assimilated and experienced that it becomes passion...." (1971, p. 349). Authentic revolution is, of necessity, a long-term process, but one that can begin at anytime i.e., whenever and wherever a group of people democratically agree to collectively engage in critical/revolutionary praxis. In other words, it can begin as an act of preparation in a political organisation, a social movement or even in a family or a classroom. Marx's efforts to expose the true nature of capitalism as well as the origin and nature of bourgeois (capitalist) consciousness were, undoubtedly, aimed at initiating and sustaining, in a critical manner, this long process of revolution, of self and social transformation (Marx and Engels, 1846: 1976, p. 60) (Marx, 1853: 1979, pp. 402-403).

MARX'S TARGETS: INVERSIONS & SEPARATIONS IN THOUGHT & PRACTICE

The struggle to transform one's objectivity and subjectivity, one's consciousness, through critical/revolutionary praxis is a constant struggle because, at present, we all exist primarily within the capitalist social relations that give rise to distorted forms of consciousness. However, this struggle can be facilitated if people recognise the characteristics of consciousness, which are produced within the uncritical/reproductive praxis of capitalism. Marx examines, and frequently parodies, these characteristics of bourgeois consciousness as he explains their material origin throughout Volumes 1-3 of *Capital*. Moreover, in Volume 4 of *Capital*, i.e., the three volumes of *Theories of Surplus Value*, he delivers a systematic and unrelenting critique of these characteristics as exhibited in the writings of both bourgeois and socialist political economists (Marx, 1863,a, b, c: 1963,a; 1968,b; 1971,c). Every characteristic that Marx criticises shares a common feature, which Marx describes as the 'violence of abstraction'. When one's thinking reproduces the separation of the opposites that constitute a unity of opposites, an internal relation, when it "violently abstracts", it distorts one's understanding (Marx, 1865:1981, p.268; see also Sayer, 1987). Of course, when this takes place in thought, it is because it also takes place in one's sensuous experience of capitalist reality. Therefore, before considering each of the negative characteristics of bourgeois consciousness, it is important to consider two aspects of sensuous experience within capitalism, which, in the absence of critical/revolutionary praxis, continuously generate these distortions.

I begin with the human practice that Marx critiqued even before he had discovered the laws of capitalism and one that he continued to critique thereafter, a practice he called alienation (Marx, 1844a:1972; Marx, 1867:1976, p. 990). This is not the pathological condition sometimes diagnosed in individuals but rather a description of normal practice within capitalist relations; however, it is possible that in extreme cases the latter might have a bearing on the former. As mentioned at the beginning of this chapter, Marx thought that all human beings should be engaged in a continuous process of becoming, i.e., a process of developing and extending all of their capacities and potentials. In capitalist societies, however, it is normal for people to alienate their potentials, or in Marx's terms, their powers, to surrender them, or give them up, to other people and/or things. The best example is when workers alienate their powers, their capacities, to create material wealth, i.e., use-values, to capitalists, who extort these powers in order to generate, with the self-same powers of labour, the value-form of wealth. Once alienated, the workers' powers are then manifested in people (capitalists) and objects (capital) that dominate and subjugate the workers (p. 1003).

In one of his earliest publications (1843:1977), Marx critiques another example of alienating practice, which is characteristic of liberal democracies, the form of government most conducive to capitalism. In this form of democracy, citizens alienate their political power and capacities by handing them over to elected representatives, over whom they have little or no day-to-day influence or control.

In other words, their political powers are exercised only in the act of voting, and once this has taken place, so too has the alienation of these powers. Marx advocated a much more direct form of democracy such as the one experienced in the short-lived Paris Commune of 1871 (Marx, 1871:1977). In this form of democracy, citizens "reabsorb" their political powers rather than alienating them in the state or political representatives (Marx, 1843:1977). Furthermore, the entire community is responsible for directing the course of society, and whenever it is necessary to delegate powers, or the execution of powers, delegates are considered to be doing work just like any other member of the community. Most importantly, these delegates are subject to immediate recall, if they fail to carry out the wishes of those who actually hold the power, viz., the ordinary citizens (1871:1977).

Although Marx does not write specifically about the second practice that underpins the violence of abstraction in the focussed way that he writes about alienation, it is integral to his explanation of capital. If thought tends to separate that which only can be properly understood as a relation, it is because we tend to experience the internally related opposites at different times and in different places/spaces (e.g. Marx, 1858: 1973, pp. 148-149; 1865:1981, pp. 966-967). To understand this, we need only consider the essence of capitalism. Even though we regularly experience the dialectical contradictions, internal relations, that constitute the essence of capital/capitalism as well as the concrete forms that develop out of this essence, e.g., commodities, we do so in a way that produces distortions in our consciousness. Our engagements with or within the opposites in the labour-capital relation (dialectical contradiction 1) rarely involve both opposites at the same time or in the same space. Likewise, any experience we have (engagement in or observation of) production and circulation/exchange (dialectical contradiction 2) is separated both temporally and spatially. It is therefore extremely difficult to intellectually grasp their unity, their internally related nature (p. 967). It is even worse with the forms that result from these internal relations. As mentioned previously, the forms exist for us in ways that totally mask their relational origin, and in the absence of Marx's scientific/dialectical analysis of capitalism, there is no possibility of discovering their origin or of tracing their development into the actual forms we encounter and experience. It is important to recognise that both of these practices, which tend to distort our consciousness, arise directly from the dialectical nature of capitalism; therefore, they cannot be overcome by anything other than the abolition of capitalism. However, they can be countered and challenged through critical/revolutionary praxis, especially as applied in, what I have called elsewhere, abbreviated experiences of attempting to engage in transformed social relations (see Allman, 1999; 2001 and Chapter 3 of this text).

As indicated above, dichotomised thinking is one of the most pervasive forms of distorted consciousness related to the sensuous experience of capitalist reality, a reality comprised of dialectical contradictions the components of which are rarely experienced and thus thought of as related. This type of thinking involves separation but not always a separation that arises from experiencing related opposites in different spatial and temporal dimensions. When dichotomising occurs, it expresses the logical impossibility of some thing, person or event being both A and not A. For example, some entity could not be both capital and not capital. Therefore, according to this abstract form of logic, which is very conducive to capitalism and which underpins dichotomised thinking, there is a tendency to conceptualise every aspect of reality, including aspects that are internally related, in either/or terms. There are abundant examples of dichotomised thinking, many of which pertain to human beings. Here I cite only a few: some object, event or person is either good or bad; one is either a teacher or a student; a person is either intelligent or practical and either labour or capital produce the value-form of wealth (rather than labour within its internal relation with capital).

Reification also characterises the consciousness of people engaged in uncritical/ reproductive praxis. With this type of thinking, people and social relations are converted into things, they are reified, and in an alternative form, i.e., personification, things are actually converted into persons (Marx, 1867: 1976, pp. 209, 1003, 1054-56). Marx particularly and most vehemently criticised the reification of capital, i.e., mistaking a social relation for a thing that actually results from the social relation. Reification, however, also characterises bourgeois thought more generally. For example, it often occurs in speech or writing when the perpetrator is seeking an economy of words; accordingly, one might write: 'Chapter 2 explains the origin of consciousness'. To correct the reification, of course, takes more words, and some people might say why bother. Ultimately, however, reification distorts the truth of reality, thereby thwarting our ability to critically understand it; therefore it is important to challenge this tendency even in our personal communication. It goes without saying, perhaps, that reification also frequently involves an improper use of the English language.

More insidiously, reification frequently develops into a form of distortion where the attributes and powers, the essence, of the person or social relation appear as natural, intrinsic, attributes or powers of the 'thing'. When this happens, thinking becomes fetishised, or in Marx's terms, fetishism attaches to the 'thing' (p. 165). Accordingly, social relations between people are misconstrued as relations between things. Fetishism is the ultimate objective and subjective expression of alienation in human practice, i.e., it is the internally related opposite of alienation, and it is the characteristic of consciousness that receives Marx's most severe vilification. In particular, he criticises the fetishism that attaches to the products of labour as soon as they are exchanged as commodities (pp. 163-177). With all commodities, the exchange-value appears to be the result of some quality intrinsic to its use-value. The clearest example of this is the money commodity, i.e., the commodity that becomes the universal equivalent and thus exchangeable for all other commodities (in Marx's time, normally actual gold and silver rather than representative paper notes). Forgetting that gold and silver are extracted from the earth by human labour in the socially necessary labour-time that determines their current value, people imagine that the value of these precious metals emanates from their natural attributes. Accordingly, people develop a strong desire for the money commodity totally ignorant of the fact that, within capitalist social relations, the constitution of its value is just as commonplace as the constitution of the value of a cow or a sack of potatoes.

For Marx, fetishism reaches its apogee with interest-bearing capital. This form of capital, money capital, appears to breed an augmented value (Marx, 1865: 1981, pp. 515-516). At least with the capitalists' mistaken notion that profits arise from exchange, there is the intervention of a commodity between the original investment of money (capital) and the result of money (capital) with an augmented value, which might suggests a social relation. But with interest-bearing capital, there is no such suggestion because the intervention is totally removed from sight. Marx explains that money lent as capital to productive capitalists becomes augmented because the money–lender receives a portion of the surplus-value, profit, produced by living labour, a portion known as interest. Furthermore, the rate of interest on interest-bearing capital is determined by the supply and demand for this type of capital and thus the amount of augmented value that accrues to this type of capital is determined in a totally different way than with other capitals, even though the surplus-value, of which it is a percentage, derives from the same source, viz., living labour. The notion that capital is a thing (rather than a social relation) with its own innate ability to produce a value greater than itself is now complete; with "...interest-bearing capital, the capital relation reaches its most superficial and fetishized form" (p.515).

Most of the erroneous forms of thinking, considered so far, involve some form of separation, and this is also true, but in a very novel way, for conflation. Conflated thinking involves a futile attempt to eliminate complexity by taking entities that are separated and reuniting them by equating them, or in philosophical terms, establishing an immediate identity between them. Transhistorical thinking always involves conflation such as, for example, when production in feudal societies is equated with capitalist production, thus ignoring the complexity of the historically specific differences between these two very different forms of production, especially the social relations within which the production takes place. Another example would be the assumption that because a machine is normally capital in capitalist society, then the cave man's club was also capital. In the *Grundrisse*, Marx parodies the political economists who tried to conflate production and consumption such that consumption produced new needs or demand and production was the consumption of raw materials (1858: 1973). To Marx, conflated thinking was both simplistic and distorted, particularly because it encouraged people to ignore historically specific differences as well as the essential internal relations, i.e., the internally related (but not identical) nature of various entities and processes (Sayer, 1987).

The forms of distorted thinking that have just been discussed can be and are normally expressed in the ideas that comprise a single sentence or a short phrase. In the case of the final form of distorted thought, i.e., capitalist ideology, this is rarely true. Ideological thought is normally expressed in persuasive explanations or discourses. The exceptions would include certain concepts that are the lynchpins of capitalist ideology, such as freedom, equality and individualism, which have been around as long as capitalism itself. In the early history of capitalism, however, these concepts also would have been expressed in a more elaborated form because there was a need to explain new aspects of reality that as yet had not been widely or commonly experienced. For Marx, ideological thinking/consciousness, at least the type that he calls ideology, is historically specific to capitalism; it is produced by people's sensuous experience of capitalist reality, within uncritical/ reproductive praxis. Ideology serves to mask or misrepresent the real contradictions that make capitalism possible, and, therefore, by helping to perpetuate capitalism, it serves the interest of the dominant class (capitalist/bourgeois). Members of the dominant class don't knowingly formulate ideology; although from their position of dominance, they are well placed to disseminate what to them appears as natural, as common sense. The only thing natural about ideological consciousness is that it conforms to the actual separations and inversions of capitalism's real contradictions; in other words, consciousness mimics our actual experience of these contradictions because consciousness and experience are an internally related unity, praxis. Furthermore not only do we experience the opposites of the contradictions in spatially and temporally distinct ways, we also tend to think more in terms of one opposite than of the other because it tends to dominate our experience, or as Marx says, it is "noisy" and attracts our attention (1867:1976, p. 279) such that it impacts on our understanding of the very meaning of life. Furthermore, the phenomenal forms, the 'things', i.e., reified form, of capitalism's primary contradiction, viz., the labour-capital social relation, are the most common and pervasive aspects of our experience. Therefore, if ideology masks and misrepresents the truth of capitalism, it is because we sensuously experience a reality, which is itself, distorted and inverted. This is exactly why Marx said that the truth of capitalism could be discovered only through scientific analysis. Marx was equally adamant that knowing the truth would not lead to the overcoming of capitalism; nevertheless, it would be a powerful weapon in the struggle against it, i.e., an essential ingredient in what I call critical/revolutionary praxis.

As I said before, ideology is usually expressed in persuasive explanations or discourses. It is important to consider the general form that these take and why those who disseminate these discourses or explanations manage quite easily to convince or persuade people that this version of events is valid. In addition, it is helpful to consider some contemporary examples. First, however, a clarification is necessary. Not every idea, explanation or discourse is ideological. To be classified as ideology, an idea, explanation or discourse has to mask or misrepresent either the contradictions of capitalism or the preconditions and/or results of those real contradictions in ways that help to sustain and perpetuate them. For example, the division of labour is both a precondition and a result of capital's contradictions;

therefore, divisive discourses such racism, patriarchy or homophobia serve to sustain not only the division of labour most advantageous to capitalism but also, and related to this, divisions within the working class. Since ideology serves to mask and misrepresent, to distort, a reality made possible by certain dialectical contradictions, internally related opposites, it follows, logically, that the general form of ideological explanations and discourses is one that coherently links fragments and partial aspects of reality. In this general form lies the secret of why those who espouse ideology manage to convince and persuade others to accept their version of reality. Ideology seems to be valid because it draws upon aspects of experience that people know to be true. Therefore, ideology is not 'false consciousness', but it reinforces the tendency for consciousness to be partial and fragmented. To reiterate, no one need make it up; all that is necessary is to engage in uncritical/reproductive praxis within capitalist social relations. Of course, those who want to perpetuate these relations and who have a critical understanding of ideology would be in a most advantageous position to either manipulate existing discourses or to construct their own.

Before continuing with a few contemporary examples of ideological discourses, there is one final aspect of ideology to consider. As might be expected from Marx's theory of consciousness/praxis, ideological thinking is not only expressed and disseminated by the written or spoken word but also in behaviour, particularly in the way people relate to other people, species and objects; and it can be embedded in the material objectifications of people's thinking, even works of art and architecture. In Chapter 3, some of the ways in which capitalist/bourgeois ideology is manifested in our experience of education are considered.

In Chapter 1, I offered a brief discussion of globalisation as well as the discourses of neo-liberalism and globalisation that have developed in concert with the most recent phase of this ongoing and immanent process by which the contradictions of capitalism are given greater space to move and operate and are, thus, temporarily resolved (Marx, 1858:1973, p.410; 1867:1976, p. 198; 1865:1981, p. 353). During the last twenty-five years, capitalist ideological thought has been sustained and bolstered by these discourses, but as the damage and havoc to people's lives have accumulated from either being left in the wake of capital's flow or drawn into its tidal surge, a need has been created for additional discourses of persuasion. David Harvey (1989) coined the phrase "condition of postmodernity" to explain how late 20th Century developments in capitalism had shaped the new movement in academia and the arts known as postmodernism. One of the chief characteristics of postmodern thought and expression is the notion that everything is relative. In fact, the idea that there is no truth, or any universal values to which all people could agree is promoted as the new "truth", which is then linked to a celebration of human diversity. Any period of capitalist restructuring, of which globalisation is only the most recent form, is messy and appears to be directionless, even chaotic. To keep the show on the road, this must be explained and justified, and the discourse of postmodernism has been extremely effective in this respect. Interestingly, relativism is not the new phenomenon it appears to be. During previous periods of capitalist restructuring, there also has been a tendency for relativism to hold sway in academic thinking and in the arts (Hughes, 1959). Whenever relativism takes hold, whether in intellectual discourse or common sense, it serves as a straight jacket on criticism because there appear to be no criteria by which we can decide, e.g., what is right and what is wrong or distinguish justice from injustice. Postmodernist thinking was still the most prevalent trend in many areas of thinking in 2001, when the events of 9/11 sent an already inverted reality into a double back flip, ending up, as it were, still upside down and doubly inverted.

The neo-conservative discourse espoused by the Bush administration added new twists to neo-liberalism and joined forces with, or became inter-linked with, the new discourse on terrorism. Right and wrong is suddenly back on the agenda, but this time, perhaps thanks to postmodernism, these judgements are made not by any reference to principled criteria but only according to "you are either with US (i.e., good) or against US (i.e., bad). The moral outrage and indignation of US citizens has been continuously fuelled since 9/11 by a government that has mastered the dissemination of these discourses and which undoubtedly has seen how advantageous they are. Any suggestion by critical citizens or intelligentsia that there might be a connection between globalisation and also US neo-imperialism and the rage of militant Islamism has been effectively silenced, condemned as unpatriotic or simply ignored. Moreover, the new war on terror has provided ample justification for increased government spending on defence thus providing a very important and necessary life-jacket for capital. It was the increased defence spending of the late 1930's that saved capitalism from the worst crisis in its history. As explained previously, it is overproduction and over-accumulation that bring capital into crisis and these are, in part, the result of insufficient demand. Defence spending is a form of governmental, Keynesian-style demand management, which can be used to avert or at least soften the effects of these crises and reinvigorate capitalist growth. However, governmental management of demand also stifles competition, which by the 1980's most capitalists and their governments had realised was essential to capitalism's proper functioning. As a consequence of the neo-liberal celebration of competition, the only way to do an about face on increased defence spending was for some external factor to make this an unquestioned and thereby unchallenged move. As horrible as it was, 9/11, accompanied by the discourses that explained it and that justified the response, was advantageous for capitalism, now abundantly graced with an enormous upsurge in demand for both productive capital and defence commodities. But the increase in defence spending was only one advantage. I mention only briefly the advantages that were meant to accrue to US capitalism from the discourse on terrorism linking Iraq to terror and eventually even relocating the 'home of terrorism' in Iraq. Access to Iraqi oil is the obvious advantage, but there is another equally important, and

41

perhaps more fundamental, advantage that has been quite successfully masked by the discourse on terrorism.

Since the early 1970's, there has been an informal but, in effect, binding agreement between the US and OPEC (the Organisation of Petroleum Exporting Countries) that all sales of oil would be denominated in US dollars, which in turn led to the creation of what is now referred to as the petrol-dollar. This meant that every nation that had to import oil needed to maintain an account in US dollars. The result has been a consistency in the strength of US dollars, which in turn has made them a good investment, and also with the dollars at hand, an increased demand for US exports—quite advantageous, therefore, on both counts. Saddam Hussein was the first OPEC leader to break the agreement when he announced shortly after George W. Bush's first election to the Presidency that Iraqi oil would be denominated in euros rather than dollars. If other OPEC nations had followed suit, this would have had disastrous consequences for the US economy (Clark, 2005). (In fact, with the impending opening of the Iranian Oil Bourse in 2006/7, it looks as if this might happen despite the 'best' US efforts to thwart it.) Hopefully it is clear that the various discourses that comprise the most recent version of capitalist ideology offer an effective way of masking and misrepresenting what is actually taking place in the real world of global capitalism. The perpetrators of the dominant ideology have managed, to date, to convince and persuade most of the public by using complementary ideological discourses that coherently draw together and link various fragments and partial aspects of reality, which are known or strongly believed, from experience, to be true. However, no matter how powerful or pervasive the ideology is, it can only maintain its sway on popular consciousness for as long as the truths it promulgates coincide with some of the truths of people's actual experiences. As I write, there are increasing signs of chinks in the armour of the present rendition of capitalist ideology. Only time will tell whether the necessary adjustments can be made and if they can whether they can assist in saving the day (world) for US capitalist hegemony.

Before closing this discussion of ideology, I want to return to those stand-alone, single ideological concepts that are so fundamental to defining the meaning of Western democratic capitalism that they no longer require the support of discourses meant to explain and justify them, viz., the concepts of freedom, equality, justice and the individual (individualism). Marx points out that the meaning of these concepts emerged from the market-exchange of commodities, which in capitalism's infancy took place only on the margins of society (1867:1976, p.280). In discussing each of these concepts and their development from the exchange of commodities, it is important to remember that exchange and circulation are one of the opposites in dialectical contradiction 2 of capital's essence, i.e., the internal relation between the circulation and exchange and the labour-capital social relation of production.

In contrast to the conventions of feudal society, people, within capitalist relations, had become 'free' to sell their labour-power for an agreed duration of time. Furthermore, the wages paid by the employer appeared (if one remained focussed on exchange) fair because equivalent, thus 'equal' to the labour-time they purchased. Since the exchange of commodities was always to be based on the exchange of equivalents, it was considered to be fair and just, and thus the basis for all 'justice'. Finally, it was the 'individual', free of all familial or communal bonds, with only himself or herself to look to, who entered into exchange with other equally unencumbered individuals. The practices of market-exchange produced these concepts and determined their meanings in a very abstract (i.e. lacking in content) and thus limited form. For example, the only important attribute that defined the bourgeois individual was someone who was free to choose, someone with free will. Therefore, the only way that one's status as an individual could be denied was to prevent them from exercising their free choice or will. Marx thought this was ridiculous but, of course, beneficial for capitalism. He envisioned a different form of society in which people would be resplendent in attributes and rich in needs, where people's individuality and also the nature of humanity would be constantly developing, constantly becoming (e.g., Marx 1858:1973, p 325). In other words, the characteristics, the actual nature, of individuals (i.e., of human beings) and also of humanity do not pre-exist their social relations but develop, for better or worse, within these relations. One reason why these bourgeois concepts are so abstract, limited and also ideological is because they focus entirely on only one of the opposites that constitute dialectical contradiction 2. If we leave behind the experiences of circulation and exchange, or that which Marx calls the "noisy sphere", and enter the realm of production it throws a quite different light on these concepts, one which suggests why they must remain abstract and limited in content in capitalist societies (Marx, 1967:1976. p.279-280).

With our attention focussed on production, it is possible to follow Marx's argument that wage-labourers are free in a double sense, i.e. free to sell their labour, true, but only because they have been 'freed' from the land and other means of production required to produce the necessities for sustaining life (pp.272-273). This bourgeois freedom is, therefore, actually an abstract, or indirect, form of compulsion. Furthermore, all illusions that the labourer's exchange with capital in the market is based on equality and justice are shattered. Again, if we follow Marx's explanation, we can understand that the capitalists do not pay an equivalent for the labour they consume. In fact, they have no reason to purchase labour-power unless this very special commodity has the special use-value of being able to create a greater value (as measured in labour-time) than that which is contained in the wage (pp. 300-304). Finally, whether wage-labourers can actually be designated as individuals, according to bourgeois criteria, is brought into question once we examine their experience of the labour-capital social relation of production.

WORTHY OF EMULATION: MARX'S RELATIONAL CONCEPTS IN MOTION

Since all these forms of distorted consciousness arise within uncritical/reproductive praxis, it follows that the only way they can be effectively countered is through and within critical/revolutionary praxis. Just how such a challenge could be mounted, even within the current context of bourgeois education, is a question addressed in Chapter 3. In the remaining pages of this chapter, two further examples of Marx's concepts are offered as exemplars of the more fluid, dynamic and relational form of thinking/conceptualising that is required for comprehensively grasping the full complexity of capitalist reality. Indeed, Marx's concepts must move because value and capital move.

The first of these concepts, Marx's concept of class, was discussed briefly in the Introduction to this book. In capitalist societies, where bourgeois consciousness, both in common sense and academic thinking, dominates understanding, class is defined in categorical terms. Accordingly, people's socio-economic class is determined by their income level, or in slightly more sophisticated versions, by some combination of income together with vocation, life-style and/or life choices. As mentioned previously, far too many professed Marxists fail to understand Marx's concept of class. For some of these people, the labour-capital social relation of production is a property relation, i.e., one that signifies the capitalists' ownership of the means of production. Still other Marxists, while seeming to have a better understanding of Marx's relational thinking, remain off the mark because of a much too limited concept of labour. For them the only kind of labour that is related to capital is manual labour, i.e., people who produce tangible commodities. Most of these Marxists would claim that Marx did not leave a clear concept of class. However, as I stated in the Introduction, nothing could be further from the truth.

In his various discussions of the labour-capital relation as the determinant of class, Marx consistently and repeatedly refers to productive labour, and with equal consistency and persistence, he explicitly states that productive labour is any labour that produces surplus-value. Therefore, what determines productive labour is not the type of commodity produced within the labour-capital relation but whether or not the labour produces surplus-value. A considerable portion of all three volumes of *Capital* is devoted to explaining Marx's relational concept of class, to tracing the ongoing historical development of the relation and to explaining in detail how the relation functions and is maintained within the capitalist production process.

Furthermore, Marx's detailed depiction of the class relation conveys a concept of class that is fluid and dynamic. Far from shrinking in numbers, the working class, the internally related opposite of capital, is constantly expanding as more and more branches of employment are subsumed within the labour-capital relation (e.g. Marx, 1866:1976, pp. 1059-62; Marx, 1867:1976, p. 929). With the relentless onslaught of globalisation, numerous people in the developing and underdeveloped nations are being forced out of peasant production in agriculture and handicrafts and into the labour-capital relation in agricultural and industrial production as well as in the provision of services. In addition, increasing numbers of people in the developed nations are finding their work reconstituted within the labour-capital relation, wherein they too become producers of surplus-value. Marx's fluid and dynamic concept of class is predictive of this process. In Marx's detailed analyses of the history of capitalism and also of what for him was contemporary capitalism, he indicates that the processes of reconstitution and subsumption do not happen suddenly. Normally, the workforce resists these processes, sometimes violently (see Thompson, 1974). Nevertheless, capitalism evokes an incessant and seemingly unstoppable process of reconstitution and subsumption, which to date has been resisted only by people engaged in uncritical/reproductive praxis.

One other aspect of the fluidity of Marx's concept of class is that he uses different terms to refer to the polar opposite of capital. He does this in order to beckon, or encourage, us to look at the concept from another perspective, e.g., the historical, contemporary or future constitution of class. However, even before he actually analyses labour in the labour-capital relation, he uses the concept of socially necessary labour-time to formulate his Law of Value. Also and importantly, when he establishes the immediate precondition of the labour-capital relation, i.e., the form of labour, the commodity form, which enters this relation, he refers to labour-power. He uses the term productive labour both in his theoretical analysis of the production of surplus-value and in his concrete examples of the contemporary producers of surplus-value. On the other hand, when his discussion also pertains to the unemployed (who also are sometimes called 'the reserve army of labour') and/or to the people whose labour would, in the future, be subsumed within the labour-capital relation, he refers to the proletariat, which is therefore a more inclusive and also fluid, or dynamic, designation. This designation as well as the terms wage-labour and working class also include the people employed by commercial capitalists, and who labour to realise (realise rather than produce) surplus-value. Just as their employers share the same interests as the productive capitalists, these workers share the same interests, viz., the abolition of capitalism, as productive labour. These workers are exploited, but not in the same way as productive labour, and Marx is very clear in explaining the differences (e.g., Marx, 1865:1981, pp. 406-416). Whether or not any of these workers are aware of their interests, their shared interests, or their exploitation is not the point; at any rate, critical awareness, the type necessary, can be developed only within critical/revolutionary praxis, and, to date, this has been sorely lacking.

In addition to his concept of class, the other best example of the fluid and dynamic nature of Marx's concepts is his relational and dialectical concept of the social forces and the social relations of capitalist production. I mentioned in Chapter 1 that I often conceptualise and present this dialectical contradiction as the third internal relation of capital's essence. To do this, however, requires some grounding in Marx's theory of consciousness, especially his concept of ideology; therefore, given the structure of this text, it is possible only now to present this third and final constituent of capital's essence. Marx does not devote a separate volume to this contradiction as he does in the case of the other two. Instead he refers to the relation between the social forces and social relations of production throughout all three volumes of *Capital* as well as in his other writings on political economy whenever he is focussing on movements within the essence and also movements within the entire capitalist socio-economic structure (e.g., Marx, 1858: 1973; Marx and Engels, 1846:1976). Although this dialectical contradiction is often conceptualised as being located within the immediate process of capitalist production, for Marx its effects not only penetrate many other aspects of life in capitalist society but movement also takes place in the other direction with the incorporation, within either one or both of the opposites of this contradiction, of factors that seem to be external to production. However, to fully understand this, it is necessary to conceptualise the social forces of production in a much more inclusive (fluid) and dynamic manner than is normally the case.

In a great deal of Marxist literature, the social forces of production are normally equated with the means of production, the objectifications of past labour-time in machines, other forms of technology and raw materials. In addition, there is a tendency to assign primacy to either the social relations or the social forces. In other words, there is a tendency to dichotomise them such that one or the other of these opposites is credited with being the motor force that drives capitalism's development. Assigning the leading role to the social forces results in the type of mechanistic interpretation of Marx known as technological determinism. Alternatively, when the social relations are seen as primary, class struggle is considered to be the motor force of capitalist development and eventual destruction. To be fair, there are passages in Marx's texts that could be used to support both of these interpretations, but neither of these interpretations does justice to Marx's more comprehensive and complex analysis of this internal relation/dialectical contradiction.

To reiterate a previous suggestion, when Marx refers to the social forces of production, he often is conceptualising much more than just the means of production. He employs this concept to refer to anything that can be used to promote labour productivity and the further accumulation of capital. As Marx's conceptualising is always based on internal relations and dialectical contradictions, an antagonistic form of internal relation, he, accordingly, conceptualises the social relations of production and the social forces of production as an internally related unity of opposites. Within any dialectical contradiction there is movement, and this means that sometimes one of the opposites can move into the other forming an identity with it. Therefore, Marx even conceptualises the social relations of production becoming, albeit only temporarily, a social force of production. For example, it is not just technological innovation that enhances productivity, various methods of organising labour in the production process can have the same effect, from the division of labour and the antagonistic form of labour cooperation, which are immanent within capital's development and which appear early in capitalist history, to the contemporary form of labour organisation known as quality circles (Marx, 1865: 1981, p. 375; 1867:1976, pp. 443, 470, 486). This is an excellent example of how Marx uses concepts to convey the dialectical movement he discovered in capitalist reality. Rather than grasping only a single moment of the content, Marx's concepts enable one to follow the movement within the content and thus to consider every aspect of that content in a comprehensive and complex manner. For example, when considering this dialectical contradiction, Marx reveals how labour in its oppositional position to capital is temporarily drawn out of opposition and antagonism and into capital during the part of the value creating process that Marx calls valorisation, the period of time during which surplus-value is created. Thus on a regular basis but for only a limited amount of time labour becomes a social force of production and in so doing labour alienates its own powers to capital (Marx, 1858:1973, pp. 341, 364; 1867:1976, pp. 1024, 1056), an act that cannot but impact negatively on both the objective and subjective dimensions of workers' consciousness. Marx's inclusive concept of the social forces does not stop here.

Scientific knowledge, ideas and even ideology can become social forces of production. It is fairly straight forward to understand how scientific knowledge can be used to increase the number of use-values produced and thus material wealth; however, it can also be used to enhance the technological capacity to intensify labour and as a result the production of surplus-value. Moreover, when scientific knowledge is patented by individual capitalists or corporations, it provides the owners of this knowledge commodity a temporary advantage over their competitors. It is much more difficult, however, to understand how ideological thinking might serve as a productive force, capable of increasing the production and accumulation of capital.

According to Marx's theory of consciousness, people produce the ideas that are dominant at any one period of time as they engage within and sensuously experience the social relations within which they produce their lives. Therefore, the dominant ideas are internally related to movements and developments within the essence (dialectical contradictions) of capitalist reality (Marx and Engels, 1846:1976, p. 67). When people's experience of reality takes place within uncritical/reproductive praxis not only do they contribute to the development of the dominant ideas but they also are susceptible to ideological explanations of and justifications for the changes and developments that are taking place. Once again, one of the best contemporary examples of this can be found with the ideology of globalisation, which has developed in concert with the necessary displacement of capital's contradictions into the global arena where they have more space to move and develop. The ideological explanation of globalisation places working people at the mercy of global market forces by persuading them that globalisation is an inevitable and unstoppable process. This type of ideological explanation/ justification can become a social force of production to the extent that it convinces people to work for lower wages, to accept the increasing insecurity and uncertainty of employment and to adopt more 'flexible' attitudes towards working practices and life-styles. Once the ideology of globalisation is widely disseminated by the media as well as in education and training and ultimately incorporated in people's understanding of reality, it is much easier for capitalists to extort a greater amount of both absolute and relative surplus-value from their workforces. However, the persuasive power of any ideological explanation depends upon its internal relation with capitalist reality. As a consequence, the ideological explanation of globalisation will only maintain its power to persuade and thus serve as a social force of production as long as it remains internally connected to the actual movements and developments in the real world of capitalism.

As noted above, education can be a vehicle for the dissemination of ideology. In the next and final chapter, I discuss how Marx's thought has been and can be used to inform our thinking about education. Clearly, the way in which we theorise consciousness is fundamental to this thinking. Since consciousness is purported to be the most prized attribute of human beings, it is surely crucial for people to become critically aware of the processes by which it is normally constituted and also of how they might gain greater control over this constitution. This brings us back full circle to the beginning of this chapter, i.e., Marx's vision of human beings developing all their potentials, of collectively becoming more fully human and of collectively being in control of this development and thus the progressive development of humanity.

CHAPTER 2 SUMMARY

In this chapter, Marx's theory of consciousness as well as his motivation for developing it and then going on to discover the laws of capitalism are explained. Implications and logical extensions of his theory are also considered. Since Marx's theory conceptualises consciousness as internally related to sensuous human practice/experience, I suggest that it is more appropriate to think of it as a theory of praxis rather than consciousness. Furthermore, it is a theory of an uncritical form of praxis that is historically specific to capitalism, which suggests the possibility of an alternative (critical) form of praxis even, albeit on an abbreviated basis, in capitalist societies. Various limited and erroneous types of thinking, including ideology, are produced within the characteristic praxis of capitalism and each of these is examined in turn. I stress that, for Marx, ideology is a negative form of thought that arises from people's actual experiences within capitalist social relations. Finally, Marx's fluid and dynamic dialectical conceptualisation is discussed by way of two of his most important concepts, his relational concept of class and his concept of the relation between the social relations of production and the social forces of production.

CHAPTER 2 QUESTIONS

1) In what ways, if any, does Marx's theory of consciousness differ from your present or previous thinking about consciousness?

2) In your society, what is the prevailing concept of human nature? In what ways, if any, would Marx be critical of this concept?

3) How would Marx explain contemporary concepts of masculinity and femininity?

MARX ON EDUCATION

"The philosophers have only *interpreted* the world in various ways; the point is to *change* it." (Marx, 1845:1976, p. 620) With these words, Marx criticised the mechanical, unhistorical type of materialism described in Chapter 2. In this instance, I use his words as a general criticism of the majority of Marxist educational theory and theorising, a criticism that will become more specific in the course of this chapter. Both before and after Marx many socialists and communists recognised that education would be a necessary component of social transformation. Therefore, as might be expected, there has been considerable interest in applying Marx's thought within the field of education, and this interest escalated after 1960 as Marx's œuvre began to be more widely available. There also have been various attempts to devise a Marxist theory of education. Some of those who have attempted to formulate such a theory have relied solely on Marx's specific references to education (perhaps most successfully Castles and Wüstenberg, 1979). However, Marx's specific comments about education, although useful, are limited. As a consequence, a much greater emphasis has been placed on interpreting the role of education and training in capitalist societies (e.g., Althusser, 1971; Bowles and Gintis, 1976; Willis, 1977; Sarup, 1978: Sharp, 1980, 1986 and Rikowski, 1996, 1999, 2001, 2003). In fact, the majority of academic work inspired by Marx in the field of education falls under this general rubric whether it emanates from historians, political economists or sociologists of education. Another area of academic activity in education more or less mirrors one of the tendencies within 20th Century Marxist theory. During the last Century, Marxist theory developed in a reactive manner that is explained in the second section of this chapter. For educationalists, the upshot has been to focus on Marx's humanism as purportedly exemplified primarily in his early writings, especially his concept of alienation (e.g. Fromm, 1964), which, interestingly, is a concept actually discussed in almost all of Marx's work. Far too little effort has been expended in considering how the entirety of Marx's thought might inform educators' efforts to change the world, or more realistically, to collaboratively prepare themselves and others for self and social transformation.

In this chapter and also in much greater detail in (Allman, 2001), I propose a philosophical approach to education based on the majority of Marx's writings, which integrates 'interpretation' with 'change'. I contend that Marx would have scorned the idea of a Marxist educational theory because it implies that education belongs to some separate aspect of human life rather than being an integral part of the process of 'becoming', i.e., the lifelong process of developing all of our human potentials and powers. It also implies that our current existence can be understood as the sum of many separate and distinct parts rather than as a totality of inner-connected relations. Accordingly, Marx's thought offers not only a theory of our contemporary existence but also an internally related, powerful and revolutionary theory of being/becoming and knowledge/knowing, thereby providing the ontological and epistemological foundations for a philosophical approach to education. These are the two foundational components that should underpin any theory of education but which are rarely recognised or made explicit. As always with Marx, his conceptualisation of ontology and epistemology is relational. His relational conceptualisation of ontology leads to a theory of social 'being' and 'becoming', which is based on the internal relation between our individuality and our collectivity, rather than one that focuses solely on individuals. In addition, Marx's conceptualisation of epistemology pertains not just to the relational origin, constitution and nature of knowledge but also to our relation with knowledge. Marx's ontology and epistemology as well as the implications of these for both formal and non-formal education are central to this chapter. First, however, I briefly consider the ideas and the trends that have arisen within other approaches to Marxist educational theory and theorising.

MARX SPECIFICALLY ON EDUCATION

Certain principles can be culled from Marx's specific references to education. These are neither identical to nor as comprehensive as those that follow from the entirety of his writings, but they are compatible with them. Perhaps most importantly, Marx realised that at least some aspects of education appropriate for a future society should be fought for or encouraged within capitalism. This is premised on Marx's recognition that his vision of revolutionary social transformation (see Allman, 1999) is as much about struggling, in collaboration with others, to transform ourselves as it is about the struggle to transform our social and economic conditions of existence; for Marx, these two components of revolutionary social transformation are internally related and thus inseparable. Before detailing the remaining educational principles that have been derived from Marx, if for a moment in addition to education we consider training, Marx offered a prophetic critique of bourgeois practice that has long had implications for training but, which, in our own present and future, also increasingly pertains to education, especially higher education. After noting that capitalists will always seek to cut their labour costs by incorporating the functions served by highly skilled and costly labour into machinery, Marx goes on to explain that when this is not possible capitalists have another tactic up their sleeves. Whenever an area of work becomes too costly to capital because only a very few people have the required skills, capitalists societies increase the provision of training in these skills and access to this provision. Also, various tactics are devised to assure that those undergoing the training gain the qualifications that signify the acquisition of the skills. Once the skills in question are widely held by formally qualified people, then those who once commanded a high wage or salary due to these skills will do so no longer; in effect, they will have been deskilled, or as is happening in the contemporary world, deintellectualised (Marx, 1867: 1976, pp. 559-60; 1865:1981, pp. 414-15). As for the remaining principles, these have been drawn from Marx's statements regarding the strategies that could be most effectively fought for in the present. There are four that received his attention.

First, as far as possible, socialists and communists should promote and encourage any move towards abolishing the bourgeois dichotomy between mental and manual labour. In addition, they should back any move towards the integration of productive work and education/learning. Thirdly, and most inclusively, they also should support the integration of education with as many aspects of life as possible (Marx, 1867:1976, pp. 610-635; Castels and Wüstenberg, 1979). The final principle has received far less attention from those trying to devise an educational theory based on Marx's specific comments about education. It is closely related to the principle of struggling for the future within the present. Marx urged that struggles for reform within capitalism should involve the collective self-education of activists, consciously attempting to transform themselves and their social relations in preparation for the socio-economic transformations they would undertake in the future (Marx, 1853:1979, pp. 402-3).

The first three of these principles are drawn from Marx's comments about the health and education clauses of the Factory Acts (Marx, 1867:1976), which resulted from the Factory Inspectors' Reports in the first half of the 1860's. Although, as Marx comments, these 'Acts' were worded such that capitalists could either evade them or implement them in an educationally less than desirable manner, he thought they should be supported because they prohibited the employment of children under a certain age unless their productive work was integrated with elementary education. At that time, most socialists/communists were fighting for the complete abolition of child employment, especially in factories. However, Marx was more realistic in that he realised that this legislation provided the only opportunity for working class children to acquire a modicum of education, and it also was a first step toward the integration of productive work and education. The final principle referred to above is drawn from Marx's verbal rebuff, in 1850, to communists who advocated immediate revolution, which he quoted in a political pamphlet published in 1853.

Focussing primarily on the first three principles, above, plus the over-riding principle of beginning the struggle for the future within the present, socialists have tried to encourage and support a polytechnic form of education that could give concrete expression to the principles (e.g. Castles and Wüstenberg, 1979; Waugh, 1988, 1994). Theorists of polytechnic education appreciate Marx's pronouncement that the 'realm of freedom' in the future society would always be premised upon the 'realm of necessity' wherein all people would cooperatively produce everything required to meet the material needs of all human beings (Marx 1865:1981). According to Marx, in neither of these realms should people be restricted to a singular and narrow form of activity. If the necessary work were to be shared by all members of society and willingly undertaken, it would need to contribute to the realisation of individuals' potentials and thus their fulfilment as human beings. Polytechnic education, of a certain form, was required for this to become a reality. In theory, polytechnic education has three goals. It should enable people to acquire the multiplicity of skills and the variety and depth of knowledge that would assure they could produce in abundance and also that would afford them the opportunity to engage in a wide-range of productive activity. It also should aim to simultaneously enhance individuals' technical skills, their minds and their physical health and prowess. Lastly, it should prepare people to work cooperatively and to engage in cooperative decision-making not just about material production but also with regard to the creation of a new society.

These are admirable ideas, but I maintain that Marx can take us much further in our thinking about education. Before substantiating this claim, I first chart the general trends that have occurred within the predominant areas of educational theorising inspired by Marxist thought. This theorising focuses primarily on either how education serves to reproduce capitalist social relations or how it, along with other experiences within capitalist societies, dehumanises people in ways that are advantageous to capitalism.

MARXISTS—NOT MARX—ON EDUCATION

During the 20th Century and thus far into the 21st , educators seeking inspiration from Marx have tended to turn to Marxist theorists who were either trying to develop Marxist theory or challenging the dominant interpretation of Marx. Unfortunately, few have turned to Marx himself. To explain this anomalous situation, we need to briefly consider what happened to Marxism after Marx. The development of Marxist theory has been influenced and often hindered by real events. I mention only some of the most important of these events. However, first it should be noted that when considering the impact of any event on Marxist theorising, it is extremely important to remember what might be termed a non-event, viz., the uneven availability of Marx's writings in various language translations as well as the extremely lengthy period of unavailability of certain key texts, especially Marx's *Economic and Philosophical Manuscripts* (1844a:1972) and *The German Ideology* 1846:1976), which were not published until the early 1930's, and his *Grundrisse* (1858: 1973), which although available in Moscow archives was only published in German for the first time in 1939 and English in 1973. In English translation, Marx's œuvre has only been available since the 1970's.

Against this background, the first and perhaps most disastrous event was that the 20th Century began with the extremely vulgar version of Marx's thought that had been endorsed by the 2nd International of the Workingmen's Association. This endorsed version presented Marx's political economy in a mechanistic, deterministic and reductionist manner, which among other things, depicted change as the result of an inevitable sequence of economic laws. It was an interpretation that allowed no place for human intentions or agency other than behaving in accord with these 'laws'. The next significant event was the Russian revolution and after 1917 the existence of the Soviet Union, a socialist/communist state purportedly based on Marxism, which under Stalin's leadership soon developed into a totalitarian monstrosity and that was followed not many years later by Hitler's fascist totalitarian equivalent. By the 1930's, many Marxist theorists had begun to think that totalitarianism was a far greater threat to humanity than capitalism. Given this sequence of events, it is not surprising that from the early days of the 20th Century, Marxists focussed their critiques on the vulgarisation of Marx and also the Soviet Union's increasing rigidification of Marx's thought (McLellan, 1980). In fact throughout the first half of the 20th Century, this stance was adopted by various people, including, for example, Luxembourg, Lúkacs, Korsch, Gramsci and early members of the Frankfurt School/Critical Theorists, and it continued to be the position of many theorists in the second half of the Century, for example, Sartre, Marcuse, Merleau-Ponty and Ollman. Most of these people tried to reinsert concepts such as human agency and class struggle back into Marxist theory. This was done in a variety of ways but primarily by emphasising consciousness, praxis, alienation and, in several cases, the influence of Hegel's dialectic on Marx's thought. Because these emphases increasingly focussed on social 'being' within capitalism, this tendency in Marxist theorising, especially with the later theorists, has been characterised as humanistic Marxism. Humanistic Marxists have concentrated primarily on Marx's early writings, and for many years, educators who were seeking inspiration from Marxist theory found this to be the most appealing and relevant form of Marxism.

Since World War II, there has been an escalating tendency for Marxist theory to be developed by academics not directly involved in politics rather than activists/ intellectuals (McLellan, 1980). Marxist theory has also been affected by the unusually long period generally referred to as capitalism's 'Golden Age' (roughly 1948-1970). During this period of almost continuous capitalist growth and a relative weakening of the class struggle, many Marxists began to think that Marx had got it wrong and that it was possible, after all, to reform capitalism. As a result some abandoned Marxism altogether, while others looked to the theories of political economists who were trying to rework Marxist theory in terms of what they thought was a changed reality, e.g., theories such as Baran and Sweezy's ill-focused depiction of monopoly capitalism; still others, while retaining Marx, felt his ideas were only relevant to the Third World and thus to Development Studies in academia. As for those carrying on with the agency/humanist trend mentioned earlier, there has been a mounting predilection to integrate or merge Marx with either other intellectual theories, such as existentialism and phenomenology, or other theorists, such as Spinoza, Kant, Weber, Gramsci and as always Hegel. This integrative trend continued even after the entirety of Marx's work became available and has only begun to abate slightly in recent years. There are many reasons for this predilection, but I think the main problem is that theorists tended to draw on Marx's writings in a very fragmented way, for example, often relying entirely on the early humanistic writings or alternatively only his later more scientific endeavours. It is ironic that those who prefer the scientific Marx almost always begin from one of his least scientific pieces of writing, viz., the 'Preface' to his 1859 *A Contribution to the Critique of Political Economy*, where with literary poise and misplaced (premature) aplomb he attempts, unsuccessfully and uncharacteristically, to reduce his complex theory of capitalism to a one paragraph summary laden with metaphorical short-cuts. In fact, this 'Preface' seems to have provided both the inspiration and the framework for Althusser's structuralism, an alternative to humanistic Marxism, which has had a profound impact on Marxist educational theorising.

With the advent of Althusser's contributions to Marxism, structuralism became the second major trend in Marxist theory. Drawing on Marx's 1859 'Preface', particularly its metaphorical references to the economic foundation, the base, and the ideological superstructure of capitalist societies, and holding onto the idea that the base was determinant to some degree or another but at the very least in the last instance, structuralists attempted to theorise the superstructure using the same degree of rigour that Marx had used in theorising the economic base. Although Althusser's work was published in 1971, it was Bowles and Gintis' 1976 publication, *Schooling in Capitalist America*, which initially had the greatest impact on educational theory. While introducing many educators to a version of Marx's critique of capitalism, these authors presented a very deterministic and reductionist interpretation of Marx's political economy. This was not the same determinism and reductionism of the 2nd International, but instead, positivism and empiricism writ large. Nevertheless, the effects were not dissimilar. Educators could find no space for their own critical agency in bringing about a better society when educational practice and policy were suppose to be directly determined by the needs of the capitalist economy, especially the need to reproduce the social relations of capitalism. As might be expected, there arose various attempts to challenge Bowles and Gintis' correspondence/reproduction theory.

Althusser's more subtle determinism, i.e., the base as deterministic only in the last instance and the relative autonomy of the superstructure, including ideological state apparatuses such as education, was utilised in many of these challenges and became extremely influential. The resistance theory of Willis (1977) provided another type of challenge that focussed on agency, especially the agency of working class boys attempting to resist their determination. However, Willis' glorification of this resistance, in which he saw the seeds of socialist struggle, was quickly rejected by many educators, who correctly realised that the resistance Willis described contained more elements of nascent fascism than of socialism. Despite Willis' mistaken analysis, resistance theory remained influential, and Apple (1985) even attempted to produce a synthesis between correspondence/

reproduction theory and resistance theory. Most importantly, however, resistance theory and its deficiencies led many educational theorists to focus more directly on consciousness. For some this meant the integration of Marx with existentialism and phenomenology, as mentioned earlier, (e.g., Young, 1971; Young and Whitty, 1977). In other cases, including initially my own, it brought into focus the writings of Paolo Freire and Antonio Gramsci. In addition, the structuralist notion of relative autonomy, although often misinterpreted, provided a boost to Marxist cultural studies, which through the writings of Stuart Hall and associates at the University of Birmingham's (UK) Centre for Contemporary Cultural Studies and theorists such as Raymond Williams and E. P. Thompson, had a considerable impact on educators who were attempting to promote the development of critical agency. It should be noted that Marxist cultural theorists, in a similar vein to their structuralist counterparts, were attempting a rigorous theorising of culture as a complement to Marx's theorising of the capitalist economy.

By the time the extremely anti-Marxist intellectual trend known as post-modernism, together with a myriad of other post-trends, entered the scene (for a period, at least, incorporating many of the US critical theorists of education, including Peter McLaren and Henry Giroux), the debate within Marxism had become centred around the divide between the culturalists and the structuralists, especially their disagreements over the meaning of relative autonomy. Whereas the culturalists interpreted this concept positively, understanding it to mean that in the production, or 'making', of culture there was space for critical human agency, the structuralists, from whom the concept originated, maintained a pessimistic stance. For them, culture was only relatively autonomous from economic determination because there were other structures immanent in the cultural sphere that were determining in their own right, e.g., literary and linguistic structures (Bennett, et al., 1981). In case it is not immediately evident, I must point out that more than a century of Marxist theorising has produced a somewhat bewildering paradox. Throughout this period, Marxist theory has tended to depart fundamentally from Marx by ignoring the internally related nature of capitalism, i.e., the way in which the habituated practices of capitalist societies, from cultural production through to economic production, are internally related and thus shaped and determined reciprocally. Had Marxist theorists returned to Marx in the 1970's and after, when the entirety of his work was finally available, they might not be at loggerheads now.

After 1989 and the collapse of 'actually existing socialism/communism', educators who refused to abnegate Marx and/or Marxist theory (initially, e. g., Sharp, 1986, in the U.K. ; Brosio, 1990; 1994, in the U.S.) took one of four routes. Some remained firmly grounded in structuralism, others in culturalism. The third and fourth routes involved a return to Marx, i.e., the entirety of Marx's thought rather than only the early or the mature Marx. Rikowski (e.g., 1996; 2003) has undertaken a valuable critique of what he calls the 'old Marxist theory of education' and has begun to develop a new Marxist approach to theorising education/training based on analysing labour-power in capitalism. His analyses focus on the ways in which education/training practice and policy serve to meet capitalism's changing needs with regard to labour-power, capital's most essential commodity; and he also considers the ways in which capital invades and dehumanises individuals through the processes that constitute them as labour-power. The fourth route is my own as developed with various learning colleagues over many years. It is a philosophical approach to knowing and becoming and therefore encompasses many aspects of human life rather than being narrowly focussed only on education. Most significantly, it is an approach aimed at developing critical/revolutionary praxis. In the next section, I discuss the main elements of this philosophical approach. By devoting a separate section to it, I am not suggesting that it is superior to others, only that it is the approach I know best, have experienced and to which I am committed.

MARX ON PREPARING FOR SELF & SOCIAL TRANSFORMATION

The ideas presented in this section are developed in greater detail and explained more fully in *Critical Education Against Global Capitalism: Karl Marx and Revolutionary Critical Education*, 2001. In this section as well as Allman (1999; 2001), I draw upon Marx's thought together with that of Paolo Freire and Antonio Gramsci, the two people who, I contend, have gone the furthest in applying Marx in their thinking about educational practice. To cut my very long story short, I began my foray into critical education by trying to apply Freire's thought within the context of higher education but quickly realised that I could not realise Freire's intent (Freire, 1972; 1985) without a much deeper understanding of Marx. Thus began the most exciting and arduous intellectual project I have ever undertaken, and one I strongly urge others to pursue. Later, I also decided to study all of Gramsci's writings that were available in English translation. This too was a valuable endeavour, all the more so because I was able to interpret Gramsci with Marx as background and also to reinterpret Freire. Moreover, I was able to apply their thinking with increasing precision and rigour in my educational practice, thereby, in collaboration with my learning colleagues, transforming that practice into an experience of critical/revolutionary praxis.

The philosophical framework, which underpins this praxis and also Freire and Gramsci's thinking on education, is derived from Marx. Marx's thinking, his dialectical conceptualisation, begins with and adheres to his philosophy, or concept, of internal relations. As explained previously, when we conceptualise entities as internally related and focus on the ways in which within an internal relation the entities mutually and reciprocally shape and determine one another, i.e., the movement and internal development of one another, we begin to understand the world and our experiences within the world in a more complex and comprehensive manner. It was Marx's philosophy/concept of internal relations that enabled him to formulate the revolutionary theory of consciousness/praxis, which provides the foundational framework for the philosophical approach to education, that is being/becoming and knowledge/knowing, explained here. Of course, it was Marx's dialectical conceptualisation, including its most central component, his philosophy/concept of internal relations that enabled him to discover and reveal the truth of capitalist reality as well as capitalism's complicity in the formation of uncritical and reproductive consciousness/praxis.

As explained in Chapter 2 and briefly recapped here, according to Marx, consciousness and 'being', i.e., human beings' sensuous experience within their material existence, are internally related. Since this constitution is reciprocal, not only does our conscious thought derive from our activity in the world but the world, our reality, is simultaneously shaped and reproduced in accord with our consciousness. Furthermore, the reality that we sensuously experience is the historically specific reality of capitalism, and the essence of this form of socio-economic organisation is also comprised of internally related dialectical contradictions. However, it is difficult to grasp the relational nature of our reality because we tend to experience the internally related opposites of these dialectical contradictions in different spaces and at different times. As a consequence, we tend to think of the opposites as separate entities, often the dichotomised opposite of one another. Our fragmented experience of capitalism and the fragmented and partial consciousness that arises in concert with this experience provide fertile ground for ideological thought. For Marx, ideology is a negative concept that denotes a form of thinking about as well as explaining reality, which is partial and fragmented but which appears to be valid and coherent because it seems to coincide with our experience of reality.

To recap further, since Marx's theory of consciousness postulates the inseparable unity of thought and sensuous human experience, it is actually a theory of praxis, moreover, a theory of praxis that suggests the possibility of two very different forms of praxis (Kosík, 1976). One of these forms, uncritical/reproductive praxis, simply serves to reproduce the existing socio-economic relations, i.e., the world as it is; while the other, critical/revolutionary praxis, attempts to transform social relations, ultimately to negate the socio-economic relations of capitalism, in order to create the possibility for the harmonious development of all humanity. By focussing on uncritical/reproductive praxis, we can understand better how education and also many other aspects of our experience contribute to reproducing and sustaining capitalist socio-economic relations and thus to the preservation and sometimes even the enhancement of capitalism. Conversely, the possibility of critical/revolutionary praxis, as discussed further later in this section, opens up possibilities for critical agency in education and many other dimensions of our lives. Those possibilities, however, are premised upon an alternative, internally related (unity of) epistemology and ontology. These are alternative theories of knowledge/knowing and of being/becoming, respectively, which arise directly from Marx's theory of consciousness/praxis, i.e., the internally related nature of consciousness, and also Marx's analysis of the internally related dialectical contradictions that constitute the essence of capitalism.

To explain these alternative theories, I must begin by explicating the epistemology and ontology that underpin the vast majority of educational practice and policy. It is important to note that these are rarely made explicit because educators and policy makers usually do not recognise that these theories are implicit in their thinking; nevertheless, they are inescapable as one or another epistemology and ontology always underpins and is imparted through educational practice and policy. I begin with the epistemology that, paradoxically, arises from both idealism and mechanical, unhistorical materialism, which to reiterate propose theories of consciousness that appear to be diametrically opposed. The paradox is dispelled, however, if we recognise that these opposed theories of consciousness are actually produced by identical thinking processes that separate and dichotomise consciousness and material reality. Once separated, it is simply a matter of prioritising one or the other. Knowledge either results from the correct philosophical thinking about reality or, alternatively, is derived from the empirical/scientific observation of reality. In both cases, knowledge, and also truth, once grasped or derived, is basically immutable, thus transhistorical, and it is also conceptualised as existing separately and distinctly from the real world. Therefore, this knowledge is unchangeable and static (although it can be added to) and by implication so too is the basic structure of the reality to which it refers. Epistemologies always suggest the particular way in which people are or should be related to knowledge. The only possible relation to knowledge afforded by this epistemology is an acquisitive one. Knowledge is conceptualised and thus related to as a thing, often a reification, to be acquired and accumulated.

A distinct theory of being/becoming, i.e., ontology, follows directly from this traditional epistemology. In terms of either formal or non-formal education, some people (e.g., teachers or political leaders) have previously acquired and accumulated the necessary knowledge that others (e.g., students and political activists) require. The educational aim is to either didactically impart this knowledge or progressively lead others to discover it. 'Being', depending on whether one is a teacher/leader or a student/activist, is, therefore, a state of either transmitting content/process or acquiring the required knowledge, while 'becoming' is an additive process of accumulation, of increasing one's repertoire of transmission skills or of adding more knowledge.

The epistemology and ontology that arise from Marx's thought are entirely different. It is important to emphasise that these theories can be systematically translated into practice only within critical/revolutionary praxis. Marx's epistemology begins with recognising that knowledge is historically specific and also never complete or finished. Since the historically specific reality of capitalism is comprised of dialectical contradictions, there is constant tension and movement in the world we are seeking to know and understand. Moreover, these internally related contradictions produce mediations, such as the value form, which not only moves between the internally related opposites from which it has originated and the other contradictions that constitute the capitalist system but does so by metamorphosing into other forms, such as the commodity, money and capital. Even more movement occurs when the tension between the opposites mounts, ultimately reaching a point that requires either or both the spatial and temporal displacement of the contradictions. With all of this constant movement and development, knowledge/knowing must move and develop accordingly. Knowledge must be constantly scrutinised and tested rather than simply acquired. Therefore, the acquisition of knowledge is the beginning rather than the end of a particular learning effort, at which point the original knowledge might have been accepted, rejected or considerably transformed, and whether accepted, rejected or transformed always understood with a greater depth than is possible with mere acquisition. Rather than relating to knowledge as if it were a thing to be acquired or possessed, with Marx's epistemology, knowledge is a tool that we use to delve deeply into reality, and it is a tool that we constantly test in order to ascertain whether it is enabling us to develop a more complex and comprehensive understanding of the world and our existence and experiences within it. We also test it to determine whether it enhances our ability to transform ourselves simultaneously with our immediate social relations, i.e., the social relations within which we are learning. It perhaps goes without repeating that this epistemology requires us to understand that the world on which we work with this knowledge is comprised of internal relations, which can be conceptualised correctly only by means of Marx's philosophy, or concept, of internal relations—his dialectical conceptualisation..

Marx's thought, especially the epistemology described above, also provides an alternative ontology. Through this understanding of ontology, we can begin to comprehend the myriad of ways in which capitalist socio-economic relations thwart our 'being' in the present and preclude the possibility of realising individually and collectively all of our human potentials, of 'becoming' now and in the future more fully human, such that 'becoming' actually becomes humanity's vocation. Marx's ontology is rooted in his concept of human nature. Rather than human nature, for better or worse, being antecedent to social being, pre-existing our existence within historically specific socio-economic relations, it develops, as does humanity's nature, within human praxis. Therefore, even in Marx's very earliest writings, he is not positing his concepts of dehumanisation and alienation against some lost human essence but instead contrasting these states of 'being' to an alternative state of 'being', which although materially possible, is unrealisable within capitalist societies. His ontological vision was for human beings to become the critically conscious creators, the 'makers', of human history. Whenever in the entire range of his writings, he refers to alienation, with increasing depth, he analyses the historically specific ways in which human beings become complicit in their own dehumanisation. Moreover, his analysis focuses not just on the dehumanisation of the oppressed but also that of their internally related opposite, the oppressor, both of whom are estranged from becoming more fully human though in different ways.

According to Marx, human beings make themselves, and not just in the biological sense but in every dimension of their 'being'; however, thus far in history, this has not been done in a critically conscious manner nor has it taken place in conditions that people have critically chosen (e.g., Marx, 1844a:1972; Marx and Engels, 1846:1976; Marx, 1852:1979). Therefore, the process of humanisation begins with developing a critical understanding of the way in which our praxis and the world we 'make' within this praxis limits both our own, individual potential and also the potential of humanity. For Marx, the process of humanisation, i.e., of becoming more fully human, is always a collective, a social, process, perhaps best expressed by conceptualising our individuality as internally related to our collectivity, to humanity, such that the harmonious, progressive development of one is impossible unless inner-connected to the harmonious, progressive development of all (Marx, 1844b: 1977, pp. 121-22). Humanisation is a process that would occur regularly and be enthusiastically embraced in a future society; it is a process exemplified in the principle "...from each according to his/[her] ability, to each according to his/[her] need!" (Marx, 1875:1977, p. 569) Marx also envisioned the process of humanisation as the infinite vocation of human beings. In future communist/socialist societies, infinite humanisation would be a major objective, fully supported such that individuals would be able to develop all the potentials of which they were capable. People would never be confined to one specific type of work or activity, which is what tends to happen increasingly as capitalism develops, but would be able to contribute to the betterment of human society through myriad types of work and activity. When human beings eventually create a socio-economic form of organisation in which this transformed process of 'becoming' is a reality, in fact, even when they begin that creating, that 'making', in a critically conscious manner, then, according to Marx, history will have become human history, a critical and creative process of abolishing all that dehumanises and activating the continuous, infinite, process of humanisation (Marx and Engels, 1846:1976; Allman, 1999).

With Marx's epistemology and ontology as background it is possible to understand the degree to which both Freire and Gramsci derived their thinking about education from Marx. Moreover, it is possible to understand how two people from two very different historical and cultural contexts formulated educational approaches based on an identical epistemology and ontology. In general terms, Freire and Gramsci have both devised educational approaches for working with people in order to render uncritical consciousness critical, thereby enabling people to begin to become more fully human. Therefore, they both offer an authentic contribution to the development of Marx's thought. Specifically, this contribution theorises a mode of learning, an educational approach, through which educators and political leaders can work **with** people to develop critical/revolutionary praxis. It is an approach to education that operationalises Marx's epistemology and ontology and that, importantly, fully embraces Marx's admonition that "...the educator must himself/[herself] be educated." (Marx, 1845:1976, p. 619) I can best explain their ideas and mine by focussing directly on the meaning and the 'making' of critical/revolutionary praxis within the current context of capitalist/bourgeois formal and non-formal education. It is important to understand that I am not offering a methodological blueprint for applying this approach. To do so would not only be impossible but also undesirable because it would be antithetical to a philosophical approach that is intended to enable people to become the critically conscious creators of their relations and conditions of existence

Any attempt to develop critical/revolutionary praxis within the context of capitalism is motivated by the understanding that the future possibility of a socially and economically just society depends on the unity, and thus reciprocity, of self and social/economic transformation. If human beings were to postpone all of these transformational processes until some future date when capitalism collapses under the weight of its own contradictions, is overthrown by revolution or when some apocalyptic event or series of events makes possible a new beginning for what is left of humanity, then they would probably end-up repeating the past mistakes of history. How, with the present constitution of ourselves within capitalist social and economic relations, could we hope to do otherwise? Being fully aware of this, Marx warned that the struggle to transform ourselves such that we would be capable of creating a better society had to begin now and also that it would be a lengthy process (Marx, 1853:1979, pp. 402-3). Furthermore, if people did not begin the struggle soon, they might become incapable of doing so because over the long-term capitalist dehumanisation might permanently debilitate humanity. For example, Marx was concerned that the narrow, singular development of people's skills and knowledge that began with the division of labour under capitalism would, in the course of capitalist history, lead to a societal condition that, today, we might characterise as social autism, a condition wherein human beings would have become incapable of communicating or working with one another. Freire and Gramsci may not have followed the logic of Marx's analysis to this dire conclusion; but they were aware of Marx's warning as well as many of the reasons for urgently responding to it, and this motivated them to develop educational approaches appropriate for this struggle.

Critical/revolutionary praxis in current educational contexts is aimed at humanising the relation between 'knowing' and 'being', i.e., the internal relation between epistemology and ontology. Obviously, within capitalism, our struggles to develop critical/revolutionary praxis in a particular educational context, whether classroom, backroom or community centre, can only offer an abbreviated experience, a prolonged 'glimpse', both objectively and subjectively, of how in the future all people could create and experience a humanised education. Through these struggles, we are not yet creating a new socio-economic organisation of society; we are preparing ourselves to do so.

One of the initial expressions of these preparatory experiences of critical/revolutionary praxis is the struggle to abolish the dichotomy between teaching and learning, which separates people into distinct positions according to educational function and status. I cannot stress strongly enough that this involves simultaneous ontological and epistemological transformations through which the processes of teaching/educating and learning are reunited within each person in the group. When the epistemological dimension of the transformation is ignored, an authority vacuum arises in the group that will have serious consequences. In fact, this is what happens in many attempts to apply Freire that are based on misinterpretations of his ideas. Those who were formerly only teachers and who initiate this approach to education/learning do not relinquish their authority, but they do need to change their concept of and their relation to authority. Most essentially, they derive their authority from living, i.e., expressing with every aspect of their 'being', the transformations they are inviting others to undertake. Their authority also issues from their ongoing responsibility to invite, initiate and reinitiate others to the transformations as well as encouraging the continuous collective evaluation of the educational praxis. Ultimately, their authority, as well as the authority of other group members, will depend upon their relation to their own knowledge and their ability to portray this relation by assuming a type of humility with respect to their knowledge, demonstrated by a willingness and enthusiasm to question and scrutinise this knowledge in concert with others.

Overcoming the teacher/learner contradiction and the dichotomisation of teaching and learning also entails the overcoming of other dichotomies. In effect, this begins with recognising that many dichotomies are actually internally related opposites. The dichotomies between process and content and also process and objectives, or means and ends, must be overcome because every process contains and therefore imparts a content that can either complement and reflect or conversely contradict the content and/or objectives. The reverse is also true since content and objectives are derived from processes or methods that also can either complement or contradict the processes involved in critical/revolutionary praxis. Finally, the dichotomy between the acquisition of extant knowledge and creation of new knowledge must be overcome such that the educational process becomes more like a collective research process. In other words, the learning group continuously uses extant knowledge in order to create new knowledge and understandings, and the new knowledge can then be used to re-scrutinise the extant knowledge. In all these cases, overcoming involves conceptualising the dichotomised opposites as internally related and also expressing this understanding through transformed praxis.

Marx's negative concept of ideology is indispensable in the struggle to develop critical/revolutionary praxis in educational contexts. It provides a stimulus to changing our relationship to all forms of knowledge. Freire clearly expresses a negative concept of ideology and its centrality to critical/revolutionary praxis (especially Friere, 1985). However, Gramsci's concept and use of ideology is often equated with Lenin's rather than Marx's concept. I disagree with this interpretation and elsewhere (Allman, 1999) have offered a detailed analysis of his use of this concept. The gist of my argument is that Gramsci thought it was more viable to change the meaning of ideology when he used it in connection with Marx's thought, or what he euphemistically refers to as 'the philosophy of praxis'. When he refers to bourgeois ideology, he uses it to denote a system of beliefs that serves to mask the true nature of capitalist reality; however, when he uses it with reference to Marx's thought, ideology means the analysis of the origin of ideas (Gramsci, 1971, p. 376). Unfortunately, this dual usage has led to important differences in the way in which Gramsci has been interpreted. However, I am confident that Gramsci used Marx's negative concept of ideology because only a negative concept is congruent with his ideas about how political leaders should work with activists (pp. 330-1; 1977; 1978). It is essential to understand that people engaged in uncritical/reproductive praxis will be extremely susceptible to ideological explanations of reality and that even those who are attempting to engage in critical/revolutionary praxis must be constantly vigilant with respect to ideology. To reiterate, ideology is the seemingly coherent expression of real separations, or fragments, of reality and real inversions in human experience; therefore, because ideological explanations draw upon real aspects of people's experience, those who articulate them have the power to persuade people to accept, or resign themselves to, the ideological portrayal of reality. Moreover, since ideology is not only expressed in words but also often embedded in material forms and human practices, in the absence of continuous critical scrutiny, we all are extremely vulnerable. When a learning group, trying to engage in critical/revolutionary praxis, is armed with a negative concept of ideology, it has a powerful stimulus to and support mechanism for undertaking and sustaining the necessary epistemological and ontological transformations.

For those engaging in critical/revolutionary praxis, Freire's concept of the 'oppressor within', similar in certain ways to Gramsci's more inclusive concept of hegemony, is also indispensable. Freire's concept follows directly from Marx's theory of consciousness/praxis, his negative concept of ideology and his concept of internally related dialectical contradictions. In this case, Freire conceptualises the relation between the oppressed and the oppressors as an internally related dialectical contradiction, wherein, due to their uncritical/reproductive praxis, the oppressed have only one vision of what they can become, viz., the oppressors (Freire, 1972, pp. 22-3). The oppressed internalise the oppressors' ways of thinking and behaving in the substance of their desires. It is only through critical/revolutionary praxis that the oppressed (i. e., anyone whose humanisation is thwarted) can begin to envision alternative ways of 'being' and 'becoming' and also begin to purge the oppressors' substance from its embedded position within their objectivities and subjectivities, their thoughts, feelings and desires. When we invite others to engage in critical/revolutionary praxis, it is crucial to remember how deeply various elements of the dominant ideology will be entrenched in all of the members of the group. This means that initially they may refuse the invitation but also that even when they accept, various members of the group, at various times, will find it extremely difficult and also threatening to rid themselves of all of the sediment, Marx called it 'muck', that impedes their humanisation. Patience is more than a virtue in these situations; it is a crucial requirement. In addition, every effort should be taken to develop an authentic atmosphere of trust in the learning group, a point which brings me back to the importance of educators and political leaders expressing the alternative philosophy in every aspect of their 'being' because this lays the foundations for trust amongst members of the group and fosters its growth.

When discussing the epistemological and ontological implications of Marx's thought, in the previous section, I often referenced his writings from 1844-1846 because in these works his epistemology and ontology are more explicit. However, his later writings, especially the *Grundrisse* and the four volumes of *Capital*, contain some of his most comprehensive and extensive discussions of the relevant concepts and/or theories, e.g., consciousness, from which these implications arise. The difference is that in the later writings he is able to relate certain ways of thinking and of 'being' to the ways in which the internal essence of capitalism and also its concrete manifestations move and develop. Therefore, we cannot fully understand his theory of consciousness and negative concept of ideology or his epistemology and ontology without his later work.

In concluding this chapter, I make a few very general comments about the implications of Marx's thought for those working in formal and non-formal educational contexts. The transformations that are required within critical/revolutionary praxis, of the self and of the epistemological and ontological relations of learning, are deep transformations. Ultimately, they must go much deeper than just knowing and relating differently so that they become assimilated and located within our subjectivities, thereby providing the dynamic of commitment and passion to the ongoing struggle to engage in critical/revolutionary praxis. For Marx there was always something more at stake than just self and socio-economic transformation, although this 'something' clearly depends on these. What it means to be a human being and for all people to be able not only to live as human beings but also to be able to develop their potentials more fully is also at stake, but then it always has been. I reassert that this was the concern that launched and perpetuated Marx's entire intellectual project. Throughout the history of capitalism, there has been the possibility of human beings uncritically and unwittingly choosing to participate in their own and others' dehumanisation rather than critically choosing the much more arduous struggle to become more fully human—choosing to participate with other human beings in the continuous process of humanisation. With increasingly disastrous consequences, it is the first possibility—the first 'choice'—that has prevailed. To a large degree, this is because most people do not realise that, through their behaviour, they are making a choice or even that alternatives are possible so that there is a choice to be made. At the very least, Marx's thought suggests that as human beings we need to start challenging the narrow horizon within which we currently exercise our 'freedom' of choice, such as, 'freely' choosing this politician or that or the next accessory for our self adornment or that of our cars, homes and ipods, and that we mount this challenge by beginning to make some truly free and authentically human choices. I urge all educators working within democratic societies, regardless of their political persuasion, to place these choices on their curricular agenda and to also promote a full exploration, consideration and discussion of them along with their implications. To choose otherwise by ignoring or dismissing this suggestion, seems to me a repudiation of the responsibility all educators have to provide learning experiences that are both genuinely educational and also essential to the preservation as well as the deepening and development of democracy.

CHAPTER 3 SUMMARY

In this chapter, I consider the implications of Marx's thought for education. The chapter is divided into three sections. In the first of these, Marx's specific comments on education and also the role he foresaw education playing in self and socio-economic transformation are considered. In the second section, I trace the general tendencies in Marxist thought, which developed after Marx's death and which impacted to some degree on educators seeking inspiration from Marx. Finally, I discuss a philosophical approach to education, and more generally to the development of critical/revolutionary praxis in various contexts, that has been formulated from the entirety of Marx's thought. This approach was formulated in order to offer an abbreviated experience, a prolonged glimpse, of critical/revolutionary praxis. The ultimate intent is to prepare people to become committed to and engaged in the process of humanisation through the struggle for revolutionary self and socio-economic transformation.

CHAPTER 3 QUESTIONS

1) In your educational experience, either as a teacher or as a learner, have you ever experienced any practice or theory that might have been inspired by Marx? If so, please discuss it and explain why you think it might have been inspired by Marx. If not, in your experience, which educational practice or theory most closely coincides with some aspect of Marx's thought? Please discuss the practice or theory and explain why you think it coincides with some aspect/s of Marx's thought.

2) Under the neo-liberal regime of globalisation, many capitalist countries have formulated educational policy aimed at creating wider access to higher education. According to Marx, what advantages would this provide for their economies?

3) One obvious implication of Marx's thought is that all education is political. Please explain why you agree or disagree with this implied contention.

ADDITIONAL BACKGROUND ON MARX'S WRITINGS AND SUGGESTIONS FOR FURTHER READING

In the main text, there were certain of Marx's writings that I referenced but for which I did not offer any commentary or background. Six of these are extremely important texts; therefore, this essay begins with some preliminary background on their content. I then go on to discuss the authors who have assisted me in my study of Marx and whom I strongly recommend to others. Selected references to the writings of any author mentioned in this essay are cited in the indexed reference section at the end of this book.

In 1843, Marx wrote an article entitled "On the Jewish Question", which was basically a criticism of the limited nature of contemporary proposals for Jewish emancipation. However, the real value of this piece lies in Marx's critique of liberal democracy and the liberal democratic form of state that had emerged in concert with the development of capitalism. Crucially, he contrasts political emancipation with human emancipation and criticises the separation of state and civil society. Some of the elements of this critique are repeated and extended, particularly with reference to social democracy, in Marx's 1875 "Critique of the Gotha Programme". This later work is famous for Marx's statement of what subsequently came to be seen as the over-riding principle of communism, viz., "...from each according to his/[her] abilities, to each according to his/[her] needs!"(p. 569) In addition, it also contains one of the most extensive discussions of Marx's vision of a socialist/communist society. It was written as a rebuke to German socialists for being seduced by social democracy and thus the limited political rights of liberal democracy. Both of the afore mentioned texts are included in David McLellan's *Karl Marx: Selected Writings* (1977). In my opinion, with the exception of the excerpts from Marx's economic texts, this is the best single volume collection of Marx's work currently available. As for Marx's writings on political economy, I would suggest that excerpts can be very misleading and recommend that these texts must be read in their complete form. McLellan's book also contains an excerpt from the notebooks Marx compiled when he wrote his *Economic and Philosophical Manuscripts* in 1843-44 as well as important excerpts from the Manuscripts, themselves. The section of the notebooks entitled "On James Mill", excerpted by McLellan, contains one of Marx's most eloquent descriptions of humanised social relations of production (pp. 121-22). The 'Manuscripts' were Marx's first writings on economics and also contain one of his most explicit discussions of his view of Hegel's dialectic.

The fifth of these important writings by Marx was the last to be published in English. His *Grundrisse*, written during the winter of 1857-58, was a work of self-clarification. For readers interested in Marx's analytical approach, his historical, dialectical materialism, there is no source more valuable than this, and I cannot stress too emphatically the importance of reading Martin Nicolaus' excellent 'Forward' to the *Grundrisse*. Unfortunately, several Marxist theorists seem to have neglected doing this and have gone on to mistake Marx's parodies of bourgeois political economy as affirmations of his own position. This leads me to issue a general warning with reference to reading Marx, and one that underlines the importance of avoiding excerpts from his writings on political economy. Marx often uses parody, especially in the *Grundrisse* and the three volumes of *Theories of Surplus Value*, to bring out the paradigmatic differences between his own thought and the thought others. Therefore, readers must beware. In fact, only last week, I read an article in a highly regarded Marxist journal in which the author purports to be quoting Marx's words from *Theories of Surplus Value*, Part 1 but is actually quoting Adam Smith!

Finally, the sixth of these significant texts, Marx's "Resultate", was originally intended as a chapter for either the end of Volume 1 or the beginning of Volume 2 of *Capital*; it was meant to provide a summary of Volume 1 and a bridge to Volume 2. For some unknown reason, Marx decided against its inclusion. Fortunately, it is published as an appendix in the Penguin edition of *Capital*, Volume 1 referenced in this book. In these pages, Marx explains how, in the course of capitalist development, labour becomes socialised, albeit in an alienated form. He also offers further detail to his analyses of alienation, reification and fetishisation and the relation between them. Although completed in 1866 and available in Russian and German translation in 1933, the "Resultate" did not receive serious attention from Marxist scholars until the 1960's.

In the remainder of this essay, I comment on various authors who have assisted me and continue to assist me in the study of Marx. I begin with the two people who influenced my initial reading of Marx. Derek Sayer, particularly in his *Violence of Abstraction*, draws readers' attention to several mistaken interpretations of Marx, and he also stresses the crucial importance of the historical specificity of Marx's concepts. Jorge Larrain's discussions of Marx's negative concept of ideology are invaluable. He not only clarifies Marx's concept with rigour and precision but also distinguishes Marx's implicit and explicit use of this concept from the way in which it was transformed after Marx's death, especially in Lenin's formulation and that of others who have taken their lead from Lenin rather than Marx.

For the most part, I came across the remaining authors towards the end of my initial reading of Marx (once one starts, one never stops reading Marx). In a few cases, however, it was some years later. They aided my self-clarification and also confirmed some aspect or another of my interpretation. Two of these authors are prolific writers, and without reservation, I recommend everything they have written as well as their future contributions. With but one exception, mentioned below, both of these authors apply Marx's thought to either historical or contemporary studies. Ellen Meiksins Wood has applied her Marx-inspired analysis to ancient Greek democracy as well as contemporary capitalism. Democracy is usually a central focus in her writings, and she also applies Marx's concept of the relation between preconditions and results (as discussed in the Introduction to this book) to good effect in many of her studies (e.g., Wood, 1995). This author has never failed to leave me with either an entirely new or, at the very least, a more complex and comprehensive understanding of the issue she examines. She repeatedly demonstrates the power of Marx's thought when employed by an extremely capable intellect. David Harvey is the other author referred to, above. Normally type-cast as a geographer, Harvey, in my opinion, is one of the most accurate interpreters of Marx's political economy in contemporary academia. Although most well known for applying his understanding of Marx in analyses of contemporary capitalism, including current manifestation of capital in consciousness and ideology and new developments in capitalist accumulation strategies, he also has written a brilliant text on Marx's political economy (Harvey, 1999).

For readers who want further assistance with understanding Marx's method of working, I previously mentioned that this appears most explicitly in his *Grundrisse* and reiterate the importance of Nicolaus' 'Forward' to this text. In addition to these, I recommend Roman Rosdolsky's (1989) *The Making of Marx's Capital*, Volumes 1 and 2. Rosdolsky provides and in-depth examination and commentary on Marx's method in the *Grundrisse* and thus the method that led to the production of Marx's *Capital*. I must also mention the writings of Bertell Ollman (e.g., 1976; 1993) who offers extensive discussions of internal relations. Although I find his explanation less than clear, a few authors mentioned in this essay (e.g., Harvey, 1999) confirm his work. My reservations regarding Ollman probably stem from coming to the concept of internal relations through an article by Charles Tolman (1981) and also through my own analysis of Marx's dialectical conceptualisation of capitalism.

Value and the 'Law of Value' are central in and crucial to Marx's explanation of capital/capitalism; in fact, capital is value in motion. In my opinion, there are two outstanding theorists in this area. The first, I. I. Rubin (1972, originally published in Russian in 1928) may have been the only political economist in the Soviet Union's infancy that actually understood Marx. He allegedly perished in one of Stalin's purges. For anyone struggling to comprehend Marx's theorisation of value and how value relates to but also differs from price, Rubin is indispensable. More recently and with equal majesty, Moishe Postone (1996) has offered an extremely valuable interpretation of Marx's theorisation of value. Postone imparts a real sense of value in motion and enables readers to understand the way in which value in motion constitutes an historically specific, covert form of social compulsion and domination in capitalist societies.

In recommending these authors, I do not mean to imply that I concur with every aspect of their interpretations. Whereas space limitations, here, preclude any comment on the minor differences in our interpretations, I do address some of them elsewhere, viz., (Allman, 2001).

GLOSSARY/INDEX

*Please note that most of the definitions in this glossary are open-ended due to the nature of Marx's concepts, most of which cannot be fully defined outside of their relation with other concepts. When it is helpful to consider a definition in terms of other concepts and definition, readers are advised to consult the items in italics. Also, please note that only glossary items are indexed.

absolute surplus-value   The type of *surplus-value* that is extorted by extending the length of the working-day/period beyond the length of time during which necessary *value* (the wage) is created. p. 14, 48

abstract labour   Socially homogeneous *labour* that comes into existence once all production takes place solely for the purpose of exchange. It is shared by all human labour and can be expressed only in temporal terms that reflect its magnitude, i.e., in terms of the *labour-time* during which it is produced. It is the internally related opposite of *concrete labour*. p. 12, 13

accumulation   The growth/increase of *capital* concentrated under the ownership or control of a *capitalist*, a firm or a national (social) capital of a particular capitalist economy. It is spurred on continuously by the need to maintain or increase the amount of *profit* resulting from the investment of capital. pp. 20, 23, 25, 26, 41, 46, 47, 71

alienation   A process of objectifying one's creative/productive and decision-making skills/powers in objects or of transferring them, giving them over, to other people within *historically specific social/economic/*political *relations*.   pp. 35-37, 47, 51, 55, 61, 70

appearance   The concrete, observable *forms* and manifestations of *historically specific socio-economic relations*, i.e., the *essence* that underpins one's immediate experience of that which appears on the surface of society. pp. 5-7, 11, 19

capital   In general, capital is the result (viz., an augmentation of *value*) of a *historically specific* process and *socio-economic relation*, i.e. the labour-capital relation. With the *division of labour* among *capitalists*, it develops into different *forms*, e.g., productive capital, commercial capital, interest-bearing/financial capital, all of which originate and are continually reproduced from the *surplus-value* extorted by productive capitalists, i.e., those who are responsible for the production of surplus-value. Social capital is the total capital invested in a particular national economy. pp. 5-11, 13-31, 34-42, 44-47, 52, 58, 61, 71

capitalism   A socio-economic system in which all production takes place in order to produce a *profit*; that involves the continuous creation and *accumulation* of *capital* and which has an immanent tendency to develop into a global system. pp. 1-13, 15-32, 34-37, 39-43, 45, 46, 48, 52-60, 62, 63, 66, 69-71

capitalist/bourgeois   A capitalist is one who employs *labour-power* to work within the labour-capital *social relation of production* and to produce *surplus-value*; who employs labour-power to assist in the realisation of surplus-value or one who invests money (capital) in these processes or some derivative of them. Sometimes capitalists are referred to individually as bourgeois or collectively as the bourgeoisie; technically, the designation means middle-class and refers to people whose value system orients around money-making. For capitalist, pp. 13-20, 22-26, 28, 29, 34, 35, 38-41, 43-45, 47, 48, 52, 53, 63, (see also *capital; capitalism*); For bourgeois, pp. 1, 2, 6, 9, 10, 19, 34, 35, 37, 39, 40, 43, 44, 52, 53, 63, 65, 70

class   A form of socio-economic existence that arises from and is determined by one's position within the labour-capital *social relation of production* thus one's role of either producing or extorting *surplus-value*. Therefore class is a relation rather than a thing. pp. 2, 3, 8-10, 34, 39, 40, 44-46, 48, 53, 55, 56

commodification/commodified   The process of transforming a specific type of *concrete labour* or a product (material object or service) into the *commodity form* thus meaning that it is produced for no other reason to its producer than to be exchanged. In the case of labour, it becomes *labour-power*. Some authors use the alternative terms commotitisation/commotitised. p. 24

commodity (commodity form)   This is a tangible product, service, event or person that assumes a *historically specific* dual form thus becoming a *unity of opposites* and in this case a unity of use-value and exchange-value, the latter of which is the appearance of *value*, i.e., is underpinned by value. pp. 5, 9, 11-20, 22, 24, 28, 33, 37, 38, 43-45, 47, 58, 61

competition   Striving against others for the purpose of gain. This activity is essential to the proper functioning of *capitalism*, especially the *Law of Value*. Initially, it involves *capitalists* trying to out-sell other capitalists who are selling the same *commodity*, but in mature capitalism it also involves the struggle to attract a finite amount of investment *capital*. pp. 6, 13, 14, 17-20, 23, 25, 28, 29, 41

concepts/ conceptualisation   Mental constructs or categories that assist one to organise and make sense of a plethora of evidence or sensory stimuli. Conceptualisation is the mental process involved in forming and using concepts. pp. 2-10, 12, 14, 16, 25, 27, 29, 30, 32, 33, 37, 39, 42-49, 47-49, 51, 52, 55, 57-62, 64-66, 70, 71

concrete labour   The *labour* that produces the use-value, the particular nature or usefulness, of a *commodity*. It is internally related to *abstract labour*; they constitute a *unity of opposites*. pp. 12, 13

conflation   A mental process, usually erroneous, that involves equating, or collapsing into one another, either distinct or *internally related* phenomena, i.e., treating them as identical thus ignoring their specificity, or *historical specificity*. p. 38

consciousness   The totality of the thoughts and feelings of which a person is aware. For Marx, it forms part of an *internally related unity of opposites* with sensuous human activity/experience thus more appropriately designated as *praxis*. pp. 3, 6, 16, 25, 31-37, 39, 40, 42, 44, 45, 47-49, 55, 57, 59, 60-63, 65, 66, 71

constant capital   Refers to the capital invested in machines, technology, raw materials and energy supplies in the immediate process of production, i.e., the production of latent *surplus-value*. Its value is based on past, or congealed, *labour-time*, and it plays no role in the creation of new *value*. Its value influences the *organic composition* of capital and constitutes part of the capitalist's *cost price*, the other part being constituted by the value of *variable capital*. pp. 15, 16, 18-21, 28

cost price   The sum of the value of *constant capital* plus the value of *variable capital*. This is what *capitalists* think constitutes the value of their *commodities* because it is what it costs them; however, the actual *value* also includes *surplus-value*, which costs the capitalists nothing. pp. 18, 21

credit   A financial mechanism that allows for commodities to be used prior to them actually being exchanged for money or capital. In capitalism, wage-labourers were the original creditors as the use-value (*labour*) of their *commodity* (*labour-power*) is used by capitalists before they receive their wages. pp. 11, 17, 21, 22, 24, 28, 29

deskilling/deintellectualisation   A process immanent in capitalism, whereby the skills/knowledge required for employment are reduced to a simpler level or the skills/knowledge become so widely spread amongst the population that their possession no longer affords power over wages/salaries and employment opportunity. p. 53

dialectical conceptualisation   Refers to Marx's revolutionary paradigm of critical thinking that he employed to intellectually grasp the internal *essence* of observable phenomena. It involves both a specific critical orientation and specific conceptual tools. pp. 2-5, 7, 9, 10, 16, 29, 48, 58, 59, 61, 71

dialectical contradiction   An antagonistic form of *internal relation*, or unity of opposites, in which one opposite is the negative because its ultimate role is to abolish the relation and thus its position of subordination and the other opposite is the positive because its role is to preserve the relation. The abolition of the relation is referred to as 'the negation of the negation'. pp. 8, 16, 27, 36, 40, 42, 43, 45-47, 59, 60, 65

dichotomies/dichotomisation   The mental process, usually erroneous, of dividing entities/ phenomena into two distinct and unrelated parts. Metaphorically, bifurcated forks in the road that must be chosen between in either/or terms. Sometimes also referred to as dualistic thinking that produces dualisms, a practice that can be confused with Marxist analysis due to the latter's focus on dualities or the dual, dialectical, and related nature of entities/phenomena. pp. 32, 36, 37, 46, 53, 59, 60, 64

division of labour   An immanent process in the development of *capitalism* whereby a labour process is increasingly divided into smaller component parts each of which is performed by a different person or group. It allows each part to be more closely monitored, regulated and controlled and usually involves a reduction in the skill required to perform each task. It is also immanent in capitalism that the various capitalist functions are sub-divided and dealt with by different persons or groups, e.g., productive *capitalists*, commercial capitalists, financial capitalists. pp. 17, 22, 39, 40, 46, 63

epistemology   The theory/study of the origin and nature of knowledge with implicit or explicit implications regarding how people should relate to knowledge. pp. 52, 59-66

essence The internal, non-transparent, substance, i.e., content, that underpins a phenomenon or system, i.e., an *appearance* . pp. 4-8, 10, 11, 16-18, 21, 36, 42, 45-47, 59, 60, 66

fetish/fetishised   Refers to a form of distorted thought (or the result of this distorted thinking) whereby the attributes and powers of a person or social relation are mistaken as the natural, intrinsic, attributes and powers of a thing. It is an extreme form of reified thought (*reification*) that becomes located in a person's desires. pp. 21, 32, 37, 38, 70

form   The result of an *internally related/ unity of opposites/ dialectical contradiction* that remains vitally connected to its source, i.e., if the source ceased to exist so too would the form. pp. 5, 8, 11-13, 15-19, 21, 24, 28, 29, 33, 35-39, 45, 60, 61, 65

globalisation   A process immanent in *capitalism* whereby various areas of the world (locales, regions and nation-states) are subsumed within capitalist relations, i.e., *social relations of production* and the commodity exchange of goods, services and *labour-power*, and ever increasing aspects of socio-economic existence are *commodified.* It is immanent because tensions build up within the *dialectical contradictions* of a capitalist economy's *essence* that can only be alleviated by displacing the contradictions in either or both time and space. pp. 9, 11, 21, 24-26, 28-30, 40-42, 44, 47, 48, 67

historical, dialectical materialism   Marx's form of *materialism*, which posits an *internal relation* between the real, or material, and the ideal (*consciousness*) and traces the development of the relation and the related phenomena/entities historically. p. 70

historically specific   Relations, things, concepts, etc. that arise and exist in their actual, or definitive, form during a specific period of history are historically specific. Conversely, those that exist across all historical periods, past, present and future, are transhistorical. Often that, which is historically specific is mistaken as being transhistorical. pp. 4-7, 10, 11, 16, 28, 29, 32, 33, 38, 39, 48, 59-61, 70, 71

human history   Marx's projection of a future period in history when human beings would collectively, consciously and critically shape and determine their conditions of existence and the future course of history, i.e., when they would be collectively engaged in critical/revolutionary *praxis*. pp. 5, 61, 62

human rights   A concept implied in Marx's writing through his critique of bourgeois rights. Human rights apply equally to the concrete needs of all human beings, e.g., the right to sustenance, housing, employment and a high level of education. Conversely, bourgeois rights (those granted and protected by liberal democracy) are abstract, formal rights that in concrete terms cannot apply equally to all people (e.g., freedom of speech, assembly and choice) because in reality positions of power and dominance allow some to exercise these rights much more freely and effectively than others. pp. 25, 69

humanisation   A collective, social process through which people continually develop their potentials in every aspect of their 'being'; therefore, an infinite process of 'becoming' more fully human. Conversely, dehumanisation refers to all political, social and economic processes that thwart or negate humanisation, or to the condition of human beings rendered by these processes. pp. 61-63, 65-67

idealism   A philosophical orientation/theory that assigns priority to *consciousness* and that views ideas, systems of ideas and often the clash or tension between competing systems of ideas as the motor force in historical change and development. pp. 31, 60

ideology/ideological   Ideas or discourses that explain reality in a fragmented and partial way and that mask or invert the *historically specific/ dialectical contradictions* of *capitalism*. It arises from people's sensuous experience of capitalist reality within uncritical/reproductive *praxis*. pp. 9, 16, 25, 31, 38-40, 42, 43, 45, 47, 48, 56, 59, 64-66, 70, 71

internal relations   A type of relation in which the related entities/phenomena mutually and reciprocally shape and determine one another and in which neither would exist as it does outside of its relation to the other. Conversely, if they were externally related, they would come together in an interaction that would produce a new but thereafter unconnected result.   No internal change in the related entities/phenomena is perceived in that which is externally related. pp. 7-11, 13, 16, 27, 30, 32, 33, 35-40, 42, 44-48, 52, 57-65, 71

labour   Marx's term for work in capitalist societies.   His most important distinction is between productive and unproductive labour.   Productive labour produces *surplus-value*, the sole basis of *profit*, and unproductive does not.   The same type of job could be one or the other; it would be productive if subsumed within the labour-capital *social relation of production*.   Also, in relation to *constant capital*, called *variable capital*. See also *labour-power*.   pp. 5, 8-20, 24, 26, 28, 29, 35-39, 42-47, 52, 53, 70

labour hour   One hour of *labour-time* that contains more or less minutes of actual labour, i.e., it is more or less porous or more or less dense. The social labour hour is the hour reflected in *socially necessary labour-time*, and it, too, can be more or less porous than in the past or future. pp. 14, 15

labour-power   This is the concept that Marx uses to designate the *commodity* that labourers sell to *capitalists* for a specified period of time.   The use-value of this commodity is *labour* and its exchange-value is the wage. pp. 12, 13, 15, 17, 21, 22, 25, 28, 29, 42, 43, 45, 58

labour-time   The measure of the magnitude of newly created *value* in a *commodity*; the time during which living *labour* impregnates a commodity with new value.   Some of this time is necessary, or paid, and thus serves to constitute the value of the wage; the other portion is surplus, or unpaid, and its duration multiplied by the *rate of surplus-value* determines the amount of *surplus-value* produced.   Note, *constant capital* only passes on congealed, or past, labour-time to the commodity's value. pp. 12-16, 18, 37, 43, 45, 46

Law of the Tendential Fall in the (general) Rate of Profit   This law identifies the recurring tendency for the *general rate of profit* in capitalist societies to fall due to *competition* (mainly to attract investment capital) driving *capitalists* to increase the *organic composition* of their *capital* investment such that relatively less living *labour* is represented in the *value* of the commodities produced. Marx identifies several counter-acting factors that account for this operating more as a tendency than an unremitting law. Note that this law refers to the general rate of profit, which can fall even when the absolute amount of *profit* rises due to *accumulation*. pp. 19, 21

Law of Value   This law states that 'the magnitude of *value*' of a *commodity* is determined by the 'labour-time socially necessary for its production'. (See *socially necessary labour-time*.) pp. 12, 45, 71

market-value   This is the average value of all *commodities* of a particular type, i.e., the sum of the average value of *constant capital* plus *socially necessary labour-time* (the sum of the *variable capital* and *surplus-value* produced by all the firms divided by the number of firms). Market-price fluctuates around market-value according to supply and demand. pp. 15, 18, 19, 28

materialism   A philosophical orientation/theory that is the converse of *idealism*. Unhistorical, mechanical materialism designates movements and changes in the material world as the motor force of historical change and development. Marx's materialism is at variance with this. (See *historical, dialectical materialism.*) pp. 32, 51, 60, 70

mediation   A *form* in motion that moves between the opposites in an *internal relation/ dialectical contradiction* and between that *unity of opposites* and others thus binding them into an integrated *socio-economic structure* of social relations, habituated practices and institutions. (See also *value/value form*) pp. 8, 24, 60, 61

money commodity/money form of value   One specific *commodity* (e.g. gold) or species of commodity (e.g. precious metals) becomes money (assumes the money *form* of *value*) when it is assumed to represent proportionately the equivalent value of every other commodity; it thus becomes the universal equivalent. To become money, the value of this commodity, like all commodities, must be determined by the labour-time socially necessary for its production, i.e., *socially necessary labour-time*. Money is the form of value that appears (see *appearance*) in exchange; it results from the exchange of commodities. pp. 12, 13, 17, 21-24, 26, 28, 37, 38, 61

neo-liberalism   The *ideological* discourse that explains and serves as a justification for the present stage of capitalist development; therefore, it is related to *globalisation*. It purports that free market exchange and competition are the ethical bases that can guide all human action. pp. 25, 40, 41

ontology   The theory/study of the nature of being/becoming thus of the human condition and human experience, how it was in the past, how it is at present and how it could be now and in the future. pp. 52, 59-66

oppressor within   Refers to a human condition wherein the oppressed, lacking any progressive vision of what they could become, internalise the thinking and behaviour of the oppressor and thus aspire and strive to become like the oppressor. p. 65

organic composition of capital   Refers to the *value*, rather than the technical, composition of a productive *capitalist's* investments in *constant capital* and *variable capital*. Firms with a high organic composition have more invested in constant than variable capital; conversely, those with a low composition are said to be labour-intensive, i.e., have more invested in variable than constant capital. p. 18-21, 28

overproduction   A type of crisis immanent in *capitalism* wherein too many *commodities* relative to current effective demand are produced. The *surplus-value* latent in these commodities is never realised. The only remedy to this crisis is devaluation, which can take various forms, even war. pp. 16, 22, 29, 41

praxis   A concept that grasps the *internal relation* between *consciousness* and sensuous human experience, a *unity of opposites* that reciprocally shape and determine one another.   It can take one of two forms.   When people unquestioningly enter into and continue to reproduce the already existing *socio-economic relations*, they are engaged in uncritical/reproductive praxis. Alternatively, when people critically question and then seek to transform both themselves and the extant socio-economic relations or even the social relations of a given context, i.e., to engage in *self and social transformation*, then their praxis becomes critical/revolutionary praxis. pp. 32-37, 39, 40, 44, 45, 47, 48, 55, 58-67.

preconditions (presuppositions) and results   A precondition is something that is inherently and logically necessary to, or required for, a future result. Results that arise from specific, inherent preconditions can become, in turn, preconditions for other future results. pp. 5, 6, 10, 11, 13, 14, 18, 19, 21, 23, 24, 28, 32, 36, 38, 39, 45, 47, 71

price/s of production   Refers to the transformation of the *commodity's value* that occurs in fully developed *capitalism* due to the *competition* for investment *capital*. Previously, both historically and logically, the commodity's value was the sum of *cost price* plus *surplus-value*, but in the price of production, surplus-value takes the form of general, or average, *profit*, which is derived from multiplying the cost price (specific to particular firms and branches of production) by the *general rate of profit*, which pertains to the ratio between the total social *capital* invested and the total surplus-value produced in an economy. p. 19

productivity   Refers to the amount of commodities produced during a specific duration of *labour-time* with a particular investment of *capital*.   *Capitalist*s constantly strive to increase the productivity of their *labour* force because experience has taught them that this will favourably affect their *profits*. Increased productivity should cheapen the cost of each *commodity* and therefore expand effective demand, i.e., demand backed by purchasing power, but when demand becomes satiated, new markets must be found; therefore, increased productivity is one of the factors that eventually lead to *globalisation*. pp. 13-20, 24, 26-28, 46

profit/rate of profit/general rate of profit/specific or general (actual) profit
Profit generally refers to a gain, or augmentation, on an investment. In *capitalism*, it derives from living labourers' production of *surplus-value*; therefore, this is an augmentation of the value that was invested in *variable capital*, or the value that was used to purchase *labour-power*. The rate of profit is the percentage derived

from the ratio between the investment of *capital* and the increase on that amount during a specific period of time. The general rate of profit is the percentage derived from the ratio between the total capital invested/employed in an economy (the social capital) and the total surplus-value produced during a specified period of time. The actual amount of profit, i.e., specific to a firm or general pertaining to the whole economy, can be determined by multiplying the capital invested by the percentage that is either the rate or the general rate of profit. pp. 9, 13-15, 17-26, 28, 29, 38

rate of surplus-value This is also called the rate of exploitation. It is a percentage derived from the ratio between necessary and surplus *labour-time*, or wages and *surplus-value*. It is an indication of the degree of exploitation taking place. The actual amount of surplus-value is determined by multiplying the amount of surplus labour-time by the percentage that is the rate of surplus-value. pp. 13, 15, 20, 21

redistribution of surplus-value This is an effect that takes place because capitalist firms with high *organic compositions*, which produce relatively small amounts of *surplus-value* (technically the amount could be zero), can sell their commodities for the *market-value* (i.e., a price that fluctuates around this value according to supply and demand), or a value that reflects the average value composition of all the competitors producing the same *commodity*. In effect, therefore, they realise the surplus-value, or *profit*, that reflects the mean surplus-value produced rather than an amount lower than this as determined by the surplus-value they have actually produced. Note, this is an effect with real consequences rather than an actual flow of surplus-value from some firms to others. pp. 15, 18, 28

reification/personification Reification is a form of distorted thinking that expresses an inverted reality. It converts people and social relations into things. Conversely, personification is a form of distorted thought that converts things into persons or that ascribes human characteristics to things. pp. 32, 37, 39, 60, 70

relative surplus-value This is the second of two general types of *surplus-value* that is created when methods are used other than extending the length of the working-day or work period beyond the period during which the wage is created (the method for extorting *absolute surplus-value*). There are three methods used to produce this type of surplus-value. All of these lead to increased *productivity* and eventually market expansion. Marx calls the first method 'increased productivity'; it involves producing more *commodities* in a given period of time with the same expenditure of *labour*. The second, 'increased intensification' involves producing more in a given period of time with a greater expenditure of labour, i.e., in a less porous, or more dense, *labour-hour*. The third is a derivative of the other two. When increased productivity takes hold in the firms that produce labourers' necessities thus lowering the *value* of *labour-power*, this results in an increase in the *rate of surplus-value* and therefore an increase in the surplus-value accruing to all firms in the economy. pp. 14, 15, 48

restructuring   A term that refers to adjustments in particular regimes, or methods, of accumulating *capital*. These adjustments take place due to crises in the existing regime of *accumulation*. pp. 40, 41

self and social (socio-economic) transformation/revolution   An infinite and *internally related* process that is the ongoing result of critical/revolutionary *praxis* and that aims eventually to bring about a revolutionary new and more progressive *socio-economic formation* and then the continuous shaping of human socio-economic conditions through critical/revolutionary praxis. pp. 31, 34, 51-53, 58, 61, 63, 66, 67

social force/s of production   Anything that can promote the *productivity* of *labour* and the further *accumulation* of *capital*. pp. 16, 45-48

social (socio-economic) relations of production/labour-capital relation   In capitalism, this is the *internal relation/ dialectical contradiction* between productive *labour* and *capital*, i.e., the labour-capital relation. Normally referred to as the social relations of production, it is actually a socio-economic relation. pp. 5, 6, 8-10, 13, 16, 17, 24, 27, 32, 34-40, 42-48, 54, 56, 59, 61, 69

social (socio-economic) structure/formation/system   This refers to the social and economic organisation of a society, which actually is a vast network of habituated human activities and *socio-economic relations* cemented together by specific institutions, values and laws. In capitalist societies, these are also bound, or cemented, together by the *value form* acting as a *mediation* between all of the relations. pp. 1, 5, 8-10, 15, 16, 22-24, 26, 46, 56, 59, 61-63

socially necessary labour-time   The *labour-time* it takes to produce a particular type of *commodity* under the normal conditions that prevail at a particular time in a given society and to produce it with the average degree of skill and intensity prevalent in those conditions. pp. 12-15, 18, 37, 45

surplus-value   The *value* produced by productive *labour* that is surplus to, in excess of, the labour (labour-time) that is necessary to produce/reproduce the value of the wage. In the immediate production process and specifically in the part of the *value creating process* that Marx calls valorisation, *commodities* are impregnated with latent/potential surplus-value, which is only realised later in the total production process when commodities are first circulated and then, crucially, exchanged. See also *price of production, profit, rate of surplus-value* and *value*. pp. 9, 13-22, 24, 26, 28, 38, 44, 45, 47, 48

uneven development   This is a necessary condition in global *capitalism* whereby there must always be differences in the *organic composition* of *capital* between various regions and nation-states that will allow for the effect of the *redistribution of surplus-value* to take place. p. 28

unity of opposites   This refers to two opposite entities/phenomena that are joined together by an *internal relation*, thus constituted as a single whole. One opposite is positive in the sense of preserving the relation; the other is the negative in the sense of eventually abolishing the relation, an act referred to as the negation of the negation. At times and for a limited period, the negative can move into and become part of the positive (preserving the relation) at which point the unity becomes an identity of opposites. See also *dialectical contradiction*. pp. 8, 9, 11, 16, 17, 27, 28, 32-36, 39, 46, 59, 63

value/value-form The substance of value is socially homogeneous, *abstract labour*, which can only be expressed in terms of its magnitude, or as a measure of *labour-time*. This *form* arises from the labour-capital *socio-economic relation of production*. The value form is the *mediation* that binds together all the habituated practices and socio-economic relations that constitute a capitalist *social structure*. When produced in surplus by *labour*, as *surplus-value*, it becomes the source of *profit* and thus also *capital*. pp. 8, 11-22, 24, 25, 28, 29, 35, 37, 38, 43-45, 47, 60, 71

value creating process In capitalist production, the labour process has a dual nature. At one in the same time, the use-value of the *commodity* is created and also new *value* is created. The value creating process also has a dual nature. Some of the value newly created constitutes the wage, but any *labour-time* beyond this involves valorisation, or the creation of new *surplus-value*. pp. 13, 47

variable capital This refers to the part of *capital* that is invested in *labour-power*. It is one part of the *organic composition* of capital (the *value* composition), the other being *constant capital*. It is the concept Marx uses for wages when he wishes to draw attention to the organic composition of capital. See also *labour*. pp. 15, 18, 19, 20, 21, 28

REFERENCES (INDEXED)

The numbers in parentheses at the end of a reference refer to the page/s where that particular source is cited in the text. Please note, this is a limited name index in that only names referenced are indexed.

Allman, P. (1999). *Revolutionary social transformation: Democratic hopes, political possibilities and critical education.* Westport, CT: Bergin & Garvey. (27, 34, 36, 52, 58, 62, 65)

Allman, P. (2001). *Critical education against global capitalism: Karl Marx and revolutionary critical education.* Westport, CT: Bergin & Garvey. (11, 15, 33, 34, 36, 51, 58, 71)

Althusser, L. (1971). Ideology and ideological state apparatuses. In L. Althusser, *Lenin and philosophy and other essays.* New York and London: Monthly Review Press, pp. 121-173. (51, 56)

Apple, M. (1985). *Education and power.* London: Ark. (56)

Bennett, T., et al. (Eds.) (1981). *Culture, ideology and social process: A reader.* London: Batsford Academic and Education in association with The Open University Press. (57)

Bottomore, T. (Ed.) (1988). *Interpretations of Marx.* Oxford: Basil Blackwell. (3)

Bowles, S. & Gintis, H. (1976). *Schooling in capitalist America.* London: Routledge and Kegan Paul. (51, 56)

Briggs, A. (1982). *Marx in London.* London: British Broadcasting Corporation (BBC). (3)

Brosio, R. (1990). Teaching and learning for democratic empowerment. *Educational Theory*, 40 (1), pp. 69-81. (57)

Brosio, R. (1994). *A radical democratic critique of capitalist education.* New York: Peter Lang. (57)

Burkett, P. (1999). Nature's 'free gifts' and the ecological significance of value. *Capital & Class* 68(Summer), pp. 89-110. (27)

Castles, S. & Wüstenberg, W. (1979). *The education of the future: An introduction to the theory and practice of socialist education.* London: Pluto. (51, 53)

Clark, W.R. (2005). *Petrodollar warfare: Oil, Iraq and the future of the dollar.* British Columbia, Canada: New Society Publishers. (42)

Freire, P. (1972). *Pedagogy of the oppressed.* Harmondsworth, U.K.: Penguin. (58, 65)

Freire, P. (1985). *The politics of education.* London: Macmillan. (58, 64)

Fromm, E. (1964). *Marx's concept of man.* New York: Frederick Ungar. (51)

George, S. (1988). *A fate worse than debt.* Harmondsworth, U.K.: Penguin. (23)

Gramsci, A. (1971). *Selections from the Prison Notebooks of Antonio Gramsci,* edited and translated by Q. Hoare & G.N. Smith. London: Lawrence & Wishart. (34, 65)

Gramsci, A. (1977). *Selections from political writings 1910-1920,* edited by Q. Hoare and translated by J. Mathews. London: Lawrence & Wishart. (65)

Gramsci, A. (1978). *Selections from political writings 1921-1926,* edited and translated by Q. Hoare. London: Lawrence & Wishart. (65)

Hall, S. (1982). Managing conflict, producing consent. In Unit 21, Block 5 *Conformity, consensus and conflict*, D102, *Social Sciences: A Foundation Course.* Milton Keynes, U.K.: The Open University Press. (27)

Harvey, D. (1989). *The condition of postmodernity.* Oxford: Basil Blackwell. (24, 40)

Harvey, D. (1995). Globalisation in question. *Rethinking Marxism, 8* (4), pp. 1-17. (27, 63)

Harvey, D. (1999). *The limits to capital.* (new edition) London: Verso. (21, 71)

Harvery, D. (2005). *A brief history of neoliberalsim.* Oxford. Oxford University Press. (25)

Hughes, H.S. (1959). *Consciousness and society.* London: MacGibbon and Kee. (41)

Kosík, K. (1976). *Dialectic of the concrete: A study of problems of man and world.* Dordrecht, Holland: Reidel. (34, 59)

Larrain, J. (1980). *The concept of ideology.* London: Hutchinson. (70)

Larrain, J. (1983). *Marxism and ideology.* London: Macmillan. (9, 70)

Liodakis, G. (2001). The people-nature relation. *Capital & Class*, 73 (Spring), pp. 113-140. (27)

Marx, K. (1843:1977). On the Jewish question. In D. McLellan (Ed.) *Karl Marx: Selected writings.*

Oxford: Oxford University Press, pp. 39-62. (35, 36, 69)

Marx, K. (1844a: 1972). Economic and philosophical manuscripts. In *Karl Marx and Frederick Engels: Collected works*, 4. London: Lawrence & Wishart, pp. 229-346. (31, 35, 54, 62,69)

Marx, K. (1844b:1977). On James Mill. In D. McLellan (Ed.), *Karl Marx: Selected writings*. Oxford: Oxford University Press, pp. 114-123. (62, 69)

Marx, K. (1845: 1976). Theses on Feuerbach. Addenda in K. Marx and F. Engels, *The German ideology*. Moscow: Progress Publishers, pp. 615-20. (51, 63)

Marx, K. (1852:1979). "The Eighteenth Brumaire of Louis Bonaparte." In *Karl Marx and Frederick Engels: Collected Works*, 11. Moscow: Progress Publishers, pp. 99-197. (62)

Marx, K. (1853:1979). Revelations concerning the communist trial in Cologne. In *Karl Marx and Frederick Engels: Collected Works*, 11. Moscow: Progress Publishers, pp. 395-455. (34, 53, 63)

Marx, K. (1858:1973). *Grundrisse*, translated and with a Forward by Martin Nicolaus. Harmondsworth, U.K.: Penguin. (26, 31, 33, 36, 38, 40, 43, 46, 47, 54, 69-71)

Marx, K. (1859: 1980). *A contribution to the critique of political economy*. London: Lawrence & Wishart. (56)

Marx, K. (1863 a,b,c: 1963, 1968, 1971). *Theories of surplus value*, Parts 1,2,3. London: Lawrence & Wishart. (35)

Marx K. (1865: 1981). *Capital*, Vol. 3, translated by D. Fernbach, introduced by E. Mandel. Harmondsworth, U.K.: Penguin. (17,19, 25, 35, 36, 38, 40, 45, 47, 53)

Marx, K. (1866: 1976). Resultate. In K. Marx, *Capital*, Vol. 1. Harmondsworth, U.K.: Penguin. (44, 70)

Marx, K. (1867:1976). *Capital*, Vol. 1, translated by B. Fowkes, introduced by E. Mandel. Harmondsworth, U.K.: Penguin. (3, 9, 12, 26, 33, 35, 37, 39, 40, 42, 43, 44, 47, 53)

Marx, K. (1871: 1977). *The civil war in France*. In D. McLellan (Ed.) *Karl Marx: Selected writings*. Oxford: Oxford University Press, pp. 539-558. (36)

Marx, K. (1872: 1977). Preface to the second German edition of the *Communist Manifesto*. In D. McLellan (Ed.) *K arl Marx: Selected writings*. Oxford: Oxford University Press, p. 559. (10)

Marx, K. (1875: 1977). Critique of the Gotha programme. In D. McLellan (Ed.) *Karl Marx: Selected writings*. Oxford: Oxford University Press, pp. 564-570. (62, 69)

Marx, K. (1878:1978). *Capital*, Vol. 2, translated by D. Fernbach, introduced by E. Mandel. Harmondsworth, U.K.: Penguin. (17)

Marx, K. and Engels, F. (1846; 1976). *The German ideology*. Moscow: Progress Publishers. (31, 32, 34, 46, 47, 54, 62, 66)

McLellan, D. (Ed.) (1977). Karl Marx: Selected writings. Oxford: Oxford University Press. (69)

McLellan, D. (1980). *Marxism after Marx*. London: Macmillan. (55)

Ollman, B. (1976). *Alienation: Marx's conception of man in capitalist society* (second edition). Cambridge: Cambridge University Press. (7, 71)

Ollman, B. (1993). *Dialectic investigations*. New York: Routledge. (71)

Postone, M. (1996). *Time, labor, and social domination: A reinterpretation of Marx's critical theory*. Cambridge: Cambridge University Press. (14, 71)

Rikowski, G. (1996). Left alone: End time for Marxist educational theory? *British Journal of Sociology of Education, 17* (4), pp. 415-451. (51, 57)

Rikowski, G. (1999). Education, capital and the transhuman. In D. Hill, P. McLaren, M. Cole and G. Rikowski (Eds.) *Postmodernism and educational theory: Education and the politics of human resistance*. London: Tufnell Press. (51)

Rikowski, G. (2001). *The battle in Seattle: Its significance for education*. London: Tufnell Press. (51)

Rikowski, G. (2003). Alien life: Marx and the future of the human. *Historical Materialism, 11* (2), pp. 121-164. (51, 57)

Rosdolsky, R. (1989). *The making of Marx's capital*, Volumes 1 and 2. London: Pluto. (71)

Rubin, I. I. (1972). *Essays on Marx's theory of value*. Detroit: Black & Red. (71)

Sarup, M. (1978). *Marxism and education*. London: Routledge and Kegan Paul. (51)

Sayer, D. (1987). *The violence of abstraction: The analytical foundations of historical materialism*.

Oxford: Basil Blackwell. (4, 35, 38, 70)

Sharp, R. (1980). *Knowledge, ideology and the politics of schooling: Towards a Marxist analysis of education.* London: Routledge and Kegan Paul. (51)

Sharp, R. (Ed.) (1986). *Capitalist schooling: Comparative studies in the politics of education.* South Melbourne and London: Macmillan. (51, 57)

Thompson, E. P. (1974). *The making of the English working class.* Harmondsworth, U.K.: Penguin. (45, 57)

Tolman, C. (1981). The metaphysics of relations in Klaus Reigel's dialectics of human development. *Human Development, 24*, pp. 33-51. (71)

Waugh, C. (1988). Polytechnic education and vocational preparation. *Liberal Education & General Educator, 61* (Autumn), pp. 28-36. (53)

Waugh, C. (1994). Socialism and education. *General Educator, 29* (July/August), pp. 17-22. (53)

Wheen, F. (2000). *Karl Marx.* London: Fourth Estate. (2)

Willis, P. (1977). *Learning to Labour.* Farnsborough, U.K.: Saxon House. (51, 56)

Wood, E. M. (1995). *Democracy against capitalism: Renewing historical materialism.* Cambridge: Cambridge University Press. (24, 71)

Wood, E. M. (1999). Unhappy families: Global capitalism in a world of nation-states. *Monthly Review, 51* (3) [www. Monthlyreview.org]. (24)

Wood, E. M. (2003). *Empire of capital .* London: Verso. (70-71)

Wood, E. M. (2006). Democracy as ideology of empire. In C. Mooers (Ed.) *The new imperialists: Ideologies of empire.* Oxford: One World. (70-71)

Young, M. (Ed.) (1971*). Knowledge and control.* London: Collier Macmillan. (57)

Young, M. and Whitty, G. (Eds.) (1977). *Society, state and schooling.* New York: Falmer. (57)

Printed in the United States
by Baker & Taylor Publisher Services